CLASSIC
CHESS PROBLEMS

BY PIONEER COMPOSERS

CLASSIC
CHESS PROBLEMS

BY PIONEER COMPOSERS

Kenneth S. Howard

DOVER PUBLICATIONS, INC.
NEW YORK

Classic Chess Problems by Pioneer Composers is a
new work, first published by Dover Publications,
Inc., in 1970.

Standard Book Number : 486-22522-4
Library of Congress Catalog Card Number : 73-93196

Manufactured in the United States of America
Dover Publications, Inc.
180 Varick Street
New York, N.Y. 10014

Preface

IN COMPILING the material for this volume the author's primary objective has been to endeavor to provide *entertainment* for everyday chess enthusiasts, rather than to treat of technical topics that might be of interest only to a much smaller group of chess problem students. So the book does not purport to be a sketch of the development of the chess problem art, nor to be an attempt to mention more than a small fraction of its famous practitioners.

Besides reproducing many old masterpieces that may have been forgotten by today's generation of solvers, the author has included other problems he considers of outstanding significance, which he believes the reader will greatly enjoy.

The ardent problem fan may be eager to attempt to solve all of the problems without referring to the accompanying solutions. Many other readers, however, may get much enjoyment merely by playing over the solutions, particularly those of the longer compositions, from which they will get an appreciation of the marvelous ability of some of the master problemists of a bygone era. For instance, instead of spending hours in endeavoring to solve Klett's marvelous five-mover, No. 28, the reader may get ample pleasure by playing through the intricacies of the solution of this masterpiece.

Readers who may be interested in a more detailed explanation of problemistic terms and themes are referred to the author's treatise *The Enjoyment of Chess Problems*.

The author is indebted to Dr. M. Niemeijer of Wassenaar, Holland, Dr. G. Páros of Budapest, Hungary, Prof. Josef Halumbirek of Vienna, Austria and G. W. Chandler of Sutton, England for data on a number of the composers mentioned in the text.

Notation

THE NOTATION used in this volume is the *algebraic,* a modified form of what is sometimes called the *Continental* because of its use in many European countries. It is commonly used in books on problems since it is more concise and precise than is the *English* notation.

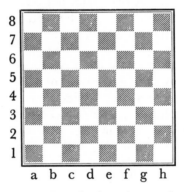

In the algebraic notation the location and moves of the men are always read from the white side of the board, or the lower side of the diagram. The files are designated "a" to "h" from left to right, and the ranks are numbered "1" to "8" reading up. Thus White's queen's rook's square is "a1" and Black's king's rook's square is "h8."

The same letters are used for the men as in the *English* notation with the exception of S (German *Springer*) for knight.

The symbol × is used for captures and the symbol ( ) for the promotion of a pawn to a piece.

The symbol *V* (version), before the name of a publication above a diagram, indicates that the position is a revision of a problem as originally published.

Contents

CLASSIC
CHESS PROBLEMS

BY PIONEER COMPOSERS

Introductory

ORIGINALLY there was little differentiation between composed endgames and problems, and manuscript collections of these are known to have been made a thousand years ago. Even up to the last century the solutions of a majority of these compositions consisted of a series of checking moves with many sacrifices of white pieces, the type of maneuvering that would be considered brilliant in a game.

One of the manuscript collections of such early problems was made in the thirteenth century by a compiler who used the pseudonym of *Bonus Socius*.

James F. Magee, Jr. (1867–1955), who founded the Good Companion Chess Problem Club in 1913, spent four years in Europe early in the century, and when in Florence became acquainted with the Bonus Socius collection, a part of which he edited and published in a privately printed volume, reproducing pages of the text and problems, illuminations and original binding. This explains how Magee came to call his chess problem club the "Good Companions" (*Bonus Socius*).

The maneuver in problem No. 1, taken from that collection, has since become known as the *Bonus Socius theme*. In the present volume this theme is also shown doubled in Otto Wurzburg's No. 111.

It probably is not commonly remembered that the great German master, Adolf Anderssen (1818–1879) actually began his chess career as a problem composer, and even in his later years he never gave up problem composition completely. No. 2 is typical of the so-called Old School style of composition, with its striking key and sacrificial moves, without much variety in the continuations.

In February, 1845, a problem (No. 3) sent to the *Chess Player's Chronicle* in England by a correspondent from India was published anonymously. The strategy involved was a novelty at

1

*Bonus Socius Manuscript
circa 1266*

White mates in two moves

2

ADOLF ANDERSSEN
*Illustrated London News
January, 1846*

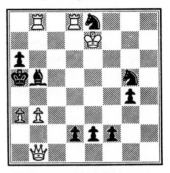

White mates in five moves

3

HENRY AUGUSTUS LOVEDAY
*Chess Player's Chronicle
February, 1845*

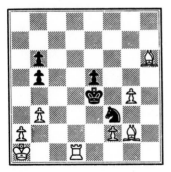

White mates in four moves

4

FRANK HEALEY
*First Prize
Bristol Tourney
1861*

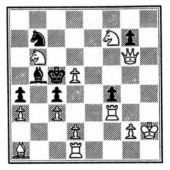

White mates in three moves

that time and the problem attracted great attention. As H. G. M. Weenink (1892–1931) stated in 1921 in his *Het Schaakprobleem: Ideën en Scholen* (which, translated into English, was issued as the 1926 volume of *The Christmas Series*, under the title of *The Chess Problem*), it "is without doubt the most famous problem ever composed."

Actually it is unsound by today's standards, since it can be solved by any initial waiting move, while after the composer's key, 1 Bc1 and Black's 1 – – Pb4, White has a choice of waiting-move continuations. If the black pawn on b6 were removed, the problem would become a sound three-mover.

The maneuver, shown in this problem, involving the move of a long-range white piece over a *critical square*, here d2, and its subsequent *masking* by another white man moving onto the critical square, releasing Black from a stalemate position, has come to be known as the *Indian theme*.

Sixty years after its publication, through the research of the English problemist John Keeble (1855–1939), the composer of the problem was found to have been the Rev. Henry Augustus Loveday (1815–1848) of the Bengal Ecclesiastical Establishment.

No. 4, composed by the English problemist Frank Healey (1828–1906), is another famous problem, its key being a pure clearance move to allow the white queen to reach g1 to mate, after playing 2 Qb1. This was a striking novelty at the time of the problem's publication, and because it was the prizewinner in the Bristol Tourney of 1861, such a maneuver has since been termed the *Bristol theme*.

The Puzzle King

CHESS PROBLEM composition in America has almost come to be regarded as having been pioneered by Samuel Loyd (1841–1911). Although there were other American composers before his day, their efforts were obscured by the brilliance of his achievements. Sam Loyd was a genius; that is unquestionable. Born in 1841 "of wealthy but honest parents," as he humorously recounted in his *Chess Strategy*, he was only fourteen when he first had a problem published, and in his fifteenth year he won a first prize in *The Saturday Courier* tourney with a four-mover, No. 5.

The major portion of his outstanding problem composing was actually done before he was twenty; in the late eighteen-seventies there was a brief revival of his problemistic activities, and then afterward he composed only occasionally, one of his last notable problems being No. 16, the prize-winner in the Novelty Tourney of the Canadian magazine *Checkmate*.

Sam Loyd's conception of a chess problem was that primarily it should be a *problem*. This penchant undoubtedly led to his lifetime occupation of the devising of puzzles, of which he made a successful business, and for which he became renowned as "The Puzzle King." His puzzles included such famous ones as "The Trick Donkeys," "The 14-15 Puzzle," "The Pony Puzzle," "Pigs-in-Clover," "Get Off The Earth," and scores of others, of some of which millions of copies were produced and distributed. He also devised the game of Parcheesi.

Alain White (1880–1951), who called Loyd his boyhood hero and kept in touch with him until Loyd's death in 1911, in describing Loyd's problem composing, wrote that "Loyd's characteristic . . . was the spontaneous presentation of themes; often he discovered them himself; sometimes he only adapted them—but it was primarily his delightful touch in passing that gave them their irresistible charm." In problem composition it was the unexpected maneuver, the "trick" as Loyd termed

5

it, that appealed to him, and as White stated, "Loyd's genius lay in making the trick in a problem striking and artistic."

Loyd himself wrote, undoubtedly having his own methods of composition in mind, "The composer thinks of some line of play that strikes him as unusual—indeed, under ordinary circumstances ridiculous—and he takes his board and men, and puzzles out some theme that will adapt itself to this curious thought of his."

No. 5 is a typical example of his early virtuosity. It is an example of what has become known as *Turton doubling*; named after a maneuver shown in a problem by Henry Turton that was published in the *Illustrated London News* in 1856, some months before Loyd's problem appeared, but which proved to be unsound. As Weenink states: "the question arose whether Turton was a correct designation for the theme at all, and whether it should not be called after Loyd. Such a claim, of course, was never pressed by Loyd himself, as he was satisfied if his problems proved puzzling to those who tried to solve them." In the Turton theme, termed a counter-clearance, a white piece (in No. 5 the queen) withdraws along a line so that another white piece (here the bishop) may move onto the line in advance of it.

No. 6 is a position where an apparently obvious first move— a "player's move"—is followed by a subtle second move, tending to lead the solver to believe that he is on the wrong track. In earlier days a checking keymove was not regarded as a serious problemistic defect, as it would be today. Undoubtedly the germ idea that occurred to Loyd was the queen sacrifice line: 1 Sg4 dis ck, Kh1; 2 Qh2 ck, P×Q; 3 Sf2, and the remainder of the problem was built around this line; 1 - -Kh3; 2 Sh2 being an excellent secondary variation.

The next composition, No. 7, is a waiting-move problem, an *incomplete block* as it is termed. A mate in two moves is *set* to follow any move of Black, except a move of the rook along the file or to g6. The key, *ambushing* the bishop behind the knight, provides a mate if the rook moves. No mate is threatened, but Black is completely *blocked*—in *zugzwang*—so that any move he may make will weaken his defense at some point and allow White to mate in the next two moves.

Loyd was fond of positions where the white king is exposed

5

SAMUEL LOYD
First Prize
Saturday Courier Tourney
New York Clipper
October 11, 1856

White mates in four moves

6

SAMUEL LOYD
First Prize
Chess Monthly
1857

White mates in three moves

7

SAMUEL LOYD
First Prize
Albion
August 7, 1858

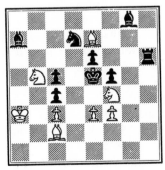

White mates in three moves

8

SAMUEL LOYD
V First Prize
American Union
1858

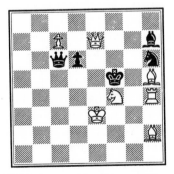

White mates in three moves

to several checks. Compare No. 8 with No. 16, in both of which the keymoves are spectacular.

The so-called "Organ Pipes" arrangement of the black rooks and bishops, as shown in No. 9, was one of the few ideas on which Loyd seemed to feel that he had a copyright, according to what Alain White wrote in *Sam Loyd and his Chess Problems*. Other composers used the same arrangement, and in fact in his youthful days the author himself employed it in a couple of problems without even being aware that Loyd, or any other composer, had previously done so, one of the author's renderings receiving fourth prize in the *Revue d'Echecs* tourney of 1904.

Loyd composed No. 10 in 1858 at the Morphy Chess Rooms and tells the story of its composition thus: "It was quite an impromptu to catch old Dennis Julien, the problemist, with. He used to wager that he could analyse any position, so as to tell which piece the principal mate was accomplished with. So I offered to make a problem, which he was to analyse and tell which piece did not give the mate. He at once selected the Queen's Knight's Pawn as the most improbable piece, but the solution will show you which of us paid for the dinner."

In earlier days it was customary to enter problems in formal tourneys under mottoes, instead of using the composers' names, in the belief that the judges would be more impartial if they did not know who the composers were. In recent times, in most formal tourneys, the tourney director may copy all the entries on some identical type of diagram and then identify them by numbers in submitting them to the judges.

Loyd had a felicitous ability for choosing appropriate or picturesque mottoes for his compositions, and used mottoes for problems even where they were not tourney entries. For No. 10 he chose "Excelsior" as a motto, undoubtedly suggested by Longfellow's famous poem, and since then where the major idea of a problem is the advance of a white pawn for several squares to promote to a piece on reaching the eighth rank, it is said to be an illustration of the *Excelsior theme*.

On No. 11 Weenink commented: "The key is the most baffling that could be imagined; the entire problem centers on that one move. The variety is small, but White's maneuvering to master the diagonal c8-h3, notwithstanding apparently dangerous checks, is splendid."

9

SAMUEL LOYD
V Boston Gazette
1859

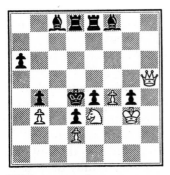

White mates in two moves

10

SAMUEL LOYD
London Era
January 13, 1861
(Second Prize Set, Paris Tourney,
1867)

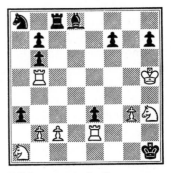

White mates in five moves

11

SAMUEL LOYD
Second Prize Set
Paris Tourney
1867

White mates in four moves

12

SAMUEL LOYD
Leipziger Illustrirte Zeitung
October 23, 1869

White mates in three moves

Again quoting Weenink in reference to No. 12: "a renowned problem. Loyd composed it during a stay in Dresden and achieved through it an immediate popularity with the German solvers. The problem is a remarkably economical treatment of the opposition-theme, a theme involving the action and counter-action of a white and a black piece. . . . Conrad Bayer (1828–1897), the greatest tourney hero of the period, called it a splendid example of strategy."

Loyd's own valuation of No. 13 was that "It is the finest problem of my book, and why? Because it contains a real four-move theme; the Queen moves from a strong position to one that threatens nothing but the leading idea, which would not be hit upon by chance. The pieces are in active play; the mating positions have all to be created, and the variations are in harmony with the theme." The judges, Jacob Elson, Benjamin M. Neill and Gustav C. Reichelm commented: "It is a colossal four-mover, and stands out grandly as the best single problem of the tournament, having a wonderfully deep design together with a most finished rendering."

In striking contrast to No. 13, Loyd's four-move master-piece, is the bizarre composition, No. 14, that he humorously dubbed "The American Indian," apparently because the bishop in making the keymove ambushes itself behind a black piece. In the early days of problem composing it was considered desirable to give problems a gamelike appearance, with approximately equal black and white forces, and so men frequently were added that took no part in the play. This practice was termed "dressing the board." But just how the black king, in a game, could have managed to wander clear across the board, with so many men still in play, is nevertheless somewhat of a mystery!

Actually the keymove maneuver in No. 14 was not original with Loyd. He employed it some three years later in an orthogonal setting, with conventional construction in No. 15. This orthogonal rendering, however, had already been shown in a problem by the eminent English composer, Benjamin B. Laws (1861–1931), that was published in 1885.

Loyd entered No. 16 in the *Checkmate* Novelty Tourney under the motto of "The Steinitz Gambit," in which White plays 5 K–K2! Alain White relates that "Few events during

13

SAMUEL LOYD
*First Prize Set
American Chess and
Problem Association
Turf, Field and Farm
1878*

White mates in four moves

14

SAMUEL LOYD
*New York Sunday Herald
1889*

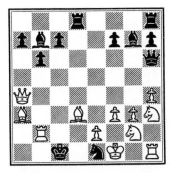

White mates in two moves

15

SAMUEL LOYD
*New York State
Chess Association
February 22, 1892*

White mates in two moves

16

SAMUEL LOYD
*First Prize
Novelty Tourney
Checkmate
1903*

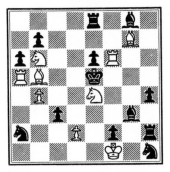

White mates in three moves

the last ten years of Loyd's life gave him as much pleasure as his winning the first prize in the Novelty Tourney of the little Canadian magazine *Checkmate*. It was the first problem tourney that I had promoted, and he responded to my request for an entry with the greatest alacrity. By return of post came the Steinitz Gambit, composed in the cars on the way down-town to his office. I was not surprised, seeing the startling originality of the theme, when the judge, Geo. E. Carpenter, awarded it the prize; and Loyd was delighted about it. . . . My account of the rapid composition of the Steinitz Gambit was generally questioned in Europe. It was decided that the problem could not be an impromptu, and that I must be very gullible to accept it as such. I mention this to show how little Loyd's genius was understood by those whom he used to call the 'careful critics.' The chief trait of his genius was its spontaneity, and this resulted, as I have explained before, in frequent inaccuracies and in occasional lack of finish. . . . I had to send the Steinitz Gambit back to Loyd twice for minor repairs, before it was completely sound."

Master of Profundity

PHILIP KLETT (1833–1910) might be called the Maharajah of what is now termed "The Old German School of Composition." As Weenink states: "The School receives its names from the fact that its precepts have for some fifty years [this was written in 1926] been those advocated in the great German periodical, the *Deutsche Schachzeitung*, the longest lived of all chess magazines, founded in 1846."

It also was sometimes called "The Continental School," since so many of its illustrious exponents were of other European nationalities. Besides such notable German composers as Johannes Kohtz (1843–1918) and Carl Kockelkorn (1843–1914), those who also composed in the "Grand Manner" included Conrad Bayer (1828–1897), Johann N. Berger (1845–1933), Konrad Erlin (1856–1944), Ottmar Weiss (1861–1942) and Max Feigl (1871–1940) of Austria; Emil Pradignat (1831–1912) of France; and J. Jesperson (1848–1914) of Denmark, to name the most outstanding ones.

In 1878 Klett edited a collection of his problems, prefaced with a discussion of the problem art, under the title *Ph. Klett's Schachprobleme*, from which the accompanying twelve compositions have been selected. Klett's booklet does not give the names of the publications nor the dates when the problems first appeared.

Klett considered the four-mover the ideal type of problem since that number of moves allowed sufficient scope for interesting maneuvering by both White and Black. He composed some three-movers and even a few two-movers—as did others of The Old German School—but he disparaged the latter because their brevity did not permit of any combination of moves.

Weenink had the faculty of expressing himself so piquantly that one is tempted to quote him frequently. Of Klett he wrote "His ideals are: difficulty, finesse, difficulty, economy, difficulty, purity of mate in the mainplays, and again difficulty!" Weenink also relates that "Klett's standard of difficulty was so high, that in many cases his contemporaries failed to solve his problems at all, a result which one may suppose was most gratifying all around!"

At this point it may be desirable to explain the terms that problemists apply to various types of mates. A *pure mate* is one where the square on which the black king stands and all the immediately adjacent ones—*the king's field*—are controlled by only a single white man or occupied by a black one. Whenever any square in a black king's field is doubly guarded, or both guarded and blocked by a black man, the mate is *impure*.

A *model mate* is a pure mate in which every white *piece* in the problem takes part, with the exception of the king, whose employment is optional. Some authorities hold that any white *pawn* used in a problem also must guard a square in the black king's field to make a mate a model, but others do not always subscribe to so rigid a tenet.

A *mirror mate* is one where the black king stands away from the sides of the board and in which none of the adjacent eight squares are occupied either by a white or a black man. Such a mate need not necessarily be a model mate nor even a pure mate, although it naturally is desirable.

A *pin-mate* is one in which there is a pinned black piece or pawn that could prevent the mate if it were not pinned.

In the three-mover, No. 17, Black's defenses are practically limited to the moves of his queen's bishop, since 1 – – B × S results in a mate in two moves. There are three model mates in the continuations after 1 – – B × Rg8, if some of the white pawns are disregarded.

No. 18 is a complex composition, but from an initial inspection it is apparent that the black king must not be allowed to flee for safety to c5. The key, however, is excellent, introducing interesting cross-checking continuations; yet only one line ends in a model mate. A *cross-check* is a check by Black which White parries by interposing a man between his king and the checking piece—"crossing" the check—and simultaneously checks the black king, either directly or by discovering check from another white piece.

An attractive lightweight, but not constructed in the Grand

17

PHILIP KLETT
Schachprobleme No. 21

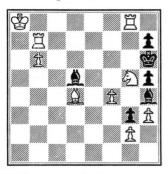

White mates in three moves

18

PHILIP KLETT
Schachprobleme No. 29

White mates in three moves

19

PHILIP KLETT
Schachprobleme No. 43

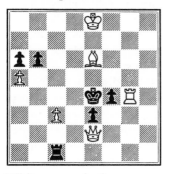

White mates in four moves

20

PHILIP KLETT
Schachprobleme No. 51

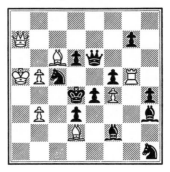

White mates in four moves

Manner, No. 19 has a good key that threatens a queen sacrifice with a mate in three moves—a *short mate* that is a model. Black's 1 – – Pb5, however, leads to a variety of play.

In composing many of his four-movers Klett employed a short threat, in No. 20 as well as in No. 19, but some of the resulting variations were often extremely subtle. In the leading line in No. 20 White's spectacular 3 Ba8 is a waiting move placing Black in a *zugzwang*. Actually the problem might be regarded as an elongation of a two-move conception, since all the thematic play follows Black's 2 – – Qg8.

No. 21 is another four-mover where Klett employs a three-move threat, followed by a quiet second-move continuation in the mainplay, with echoing knight and long-range queen mates.

The next problem, No. 22, is a waiting-move composition. White makes an astonishing keymove, to provide the mate in a single variation, and waits for Black to weaken his defenses. The trivial duals on some of the mating moves did not seem to trouble Klett, although they would have been regarded as damning defects by the old adherents of The English School of Composition, who made a fetish of accuracy.

In the attractively open setting of No. 23, again the keymove threatens a short mate in three moves. But after 1 – – Ke5 the continuation in the mainplay is not apparent, so that even if a solver hit upon the correct key, he might well believe he had made a mistake. Strategically this second white move vacates f3 so the queen may play to that square for one of the mates.

The purpose of White's maneuvering in No. 24 is well disguised, making it a difficult problem to solve. The withdrawal of the bishop from d6 threatens an immediate mate by 2 Sc7 or Sf6, but the *switchback* of the bishop after 1 – – Pc4 leads to some involved play.

No. 25 is another problem in which an immediate mate is threatened following the keymove. But the reason why the bishop should have to move to a8 rather than b7, or to some other square along the h1-a8 diagonal, requires a careful analysis of the position. White's second-move continuation after Black's odd defense, 1 – – Bb8, is a surprising one! The queen sacrifice line, ending in a model mate, may be regarded as the mainplay of this brilliant composition.

21

PHILIP KLETT
Schachprobleme No. 65

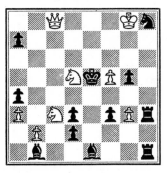

White mates in four moves

22

PHILIP KLETT
Schachprobleme No. 68

White mates in four moves

23

PHILIP KLETT
Schachprobleme No. 70

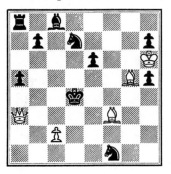

White mates in four moves

24

PHILIP KLETT
Schachprobleme No. 71

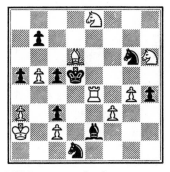

White mates in four moves

25

PHILIP KLETT
Schachprobleme No. 73

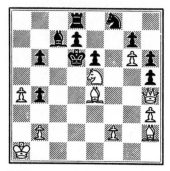

White mates in four moves

26

PHILIP KLETT
Schachprobleme No. 75

White mates in four moves

27

PHILIP KLETT
Schachprobleme No. 76

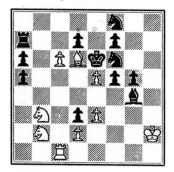

White mates in four moves

28

PHILIP KLETT
Schachprobleme No. 110

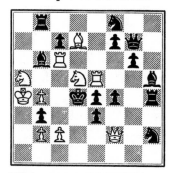

White mates in five moves

In the remarkable No. 26 not only the key but White's quiet second-move continuations in the major lines are especially obscure, and although there is a threat of mate in three moves, Black has a wide variety of defenses to prevent it. This must have been one of the most difficult problems for Klett's contemporaries to solve.

There is not much variety of defense in No. 27, but in the mainplay White's quiet second-move continuation is a most unlikely appearing move, a type of construction that Klett frequently employed, as already shown in problems Nos. 21, 23, 25 and 26, which makes the solution of many of his compositions so puzzling.

The next problem is one of the marvelous masterpieces of which Klett composed several and in the construction of which he has had no superior as a "Master of Profundity." No. 28 is an astounding achievement and it is suggested that the reader— no matter how enthusiastic a problem fan he may be—do not attempt to solve it, but to play through the ramifications of the solution to appreciate Klett's astonishing constructive ability. The solution is so complex that some of the incidental minor lines, where the continuations are apparent, have been omitted.

The Delicate Touch

PROBLEMS with a total of seven or fewer men are termed *miniatures* and their attractive appearance appeals to many chess enthusiasts, although such compositions often may prove to be more difficult to solve than those with many more men. Problems with a larger number of men frequently offer more guideposts to their solution. All of the problems reproduced in this chapter are miniatures, and in a majority of them the attractiveness of the mating positions is a dominant feature.

Among American problemists William A. Shinkman (1847–1933), Dr. Gilbert Dobbs (1869–1941) and Otto Wurzburg (1875–1951) long will be remembered for their composition of many beautiful problems with a minimum number of men.

Shinkman, "The Wizard of Grand Rapids," was the most prolific of American problemists, composing some thirty-five hundred problems, over six hundred of which were selected by him for reproduction in *The Golden Argosy*, the 25th Anniversary volume of *The Christmas Series*, for which Otto Wurzburg, his nephew, wrote the introduction.

Shinkman composed so many lightweight problems that there is a story, possibly apocryphal, that one of his admirers once made him a present of a set of chessmen, with a facetious note saying that judging from his published problems "apparently he did not possess a full set of men."

In comparing the work of Loyd and Shinkman, Alain White wrote: "Loyd toyed with themes, Shinkman masters them. Loyd's genius was a natural spring, bubbling up irrepressibly; Shinkman combines genius with a pains-taking talent, and the combination reminds one of a quarry, offering some of its product spontaneously at the surface while much of it has to be mined from below."

Shinkman studied the possibilities of pawn promotions extensively, seventy-three of his pawn promotion problems being

29

WILLIAM A. SHINKMAN
Western Advertiser
1872

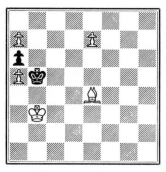

White mates in three moves

30

WILLIAM A. SHINKMAN
Dubuque Chess Journal
circa 1872

White mates in three moves

31

WILLIAM A. SHINKMAN
Dubuque Chess Journal
November, 1890

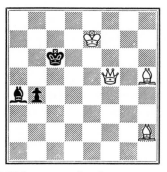

White mates in three moves

32

WILLIAM A. SHINKMAN
V Deutsches Wochenschach
January 28, 1890

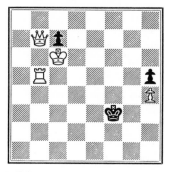

White mates in four moves

reproduced in *The Theory of Pawn Promotion*, the 1912 volume of *The Christmas Series*. In No. 29 White promotes pawns to rook, knight and queen, according to Black's play. In No. 30 the promotions are to rook, bishop and queen.

The repetition of the same type of position in two or more of the mates in a problem is termed an *echo*. Ordinarily a composer only endeavors to echo model mates. Where the black king stands on squares of the same color in each of the mates it is a *monochrome echo*; where the king stands on a white square in one mate and on a black square in another it is a *chameleon echo*.

In the brilliant No. 31 the white queen is sacrificed in two lines of play, ending in chameleon echoed model mates. Wurzburg shows a similar queen sacrifice in No. 37. An excellent key in No. 32 leads to one model mate given with the white pieces along files and another with the pieces along ranks, with somewhat of an echoing effect.

No. 33 looks like a simple affair, but to echo a model mate with a minimal white and black force requires the skill of a master. The key in No. 34 gives the black king five additional flight squares, so that he has the maximum of eight flights—a task achievement in a miniature setting worthy of "The Wizard."

Although Shinkman was not a definite disciple of the Bohemian School, of which the composing ideals are described on page 26, No. 35, with its intricate chameleon echo of a model mate, is a gem that could not be surpassed. No. 36 is another remarkable minimal problem in which the white king successfully dodges the attack of the black knight after its initial checks.

Commenting on Otto Wurzburg's compositions in *A Sketchbook of American Chess Problematists*, the third in Frank Altschul's beautiful series of chess problem books, privately printed at his Overbrook Press, Alain White wrote: "Sharply pointed keys, brilliant sacrifices, mastery of difficult combinations, originality of idea, quiet play and beauty of mate, and astonishing economy of means, all these abound in his delightful works."

Wurzburg was exceedingly versatile, his work ranging from highly complex strategic compositions to miniatures featuring model mate echoes, and he was definitely influenced by Bohemian tenets of construction. The author has always re-

33

WILLIAM A. SHINKMAN
Tiffin Tribune
circa 1898

White mates in three moves

34

WILLIAM A. SHINKMAN
Checkmate
December, 1901

White mates in three moves

35

WILLIAM A. SHINKMAN
Schachminiaturen, Volume II
1903

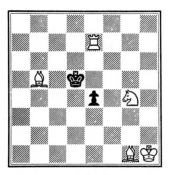

White mates in five moves

36

WILLIAM A. SHINKMAN
Lasker's Chess Magazine
June, 1905

White mates in five moves

37

OTTO WURZBURG
V Bahn Frei
1895

White mates in three moves

38

OTTO WURZBURG
Westen und Daheim
September 10, 1911

White mates in three moves

39

OTTO WURZBURG
First Prize
Samuel Loyd
Memorial Tourney
1913

White mates in three moves

40

OTTO WURZBURG
Fourth Prize
Prager Presse
1926

White mates in three moves

41

OTTO WURZBURG
First Prize
Third Cheney Miniature
Tourney
1937

White mates in four moves

42

OTTO WURZBURG
First Honorable Mention
American Chess Bulletin
1940

White mates in three moves

43

OTTO WURZBURG
First Prize
Sam Loyd Memorial Tourney
Chess Review
1942

White mates in three moves

44

OTTO WURZBURG
Honorable Mention
American Chess Bulletin
1955

White mates in three moves

garded him as the outstanding *artist* among American problemists.

No. 37 is a famous masterpiece illustrating the Turton theme,
previously shown in Loyd's No. 5. The queen sacrifice after
1 – – Pa5 is a brilliant additional feature. No. 38 is an odd
affair, really more "Loydesque" than was usual for Wurzburg.

No. 39 is typical of Wurzburg's style. The key exposes the
white king to checks by the black rook, both along the rank
and along the file, and the long-range model mate after the self-
blocking move of the rook to a1 is spectacular. While the
chameleon echoed model mates in No. 40 are not original,
the key is striking and White's quiet second moves are pleasing.

The author was the judge in the Third Cheney Miniature
Tourney and in making the award commented on No. 41:
"This beautiful composition has two pairs of chameleon echo
model mates and a third chameleon echo of impure mates.
While the mating positions themselves are familiar ones I have
never seen them shown as chameleon echoes. The problem is
a constructive masterpiece. The point of the key is accentuated
by a close try; there are no checks in any of the continuations;
and each of the four white pieces is active in the course of the
solution, the rook and each bishop giving mate in turn."

In No. 42 an excellent key is followed by a pair of echoed
model mates and a pair of echoed impure pin-mates. No. 43,
another typical Wurzburg gem, features a duel between the
white rooks and the black queen. In No. 44 the keymove gives
the black king two additional flight squares, with three of the
ensuing lines ending in model mates. This problem was published after Wurzburg's death.

The Bohemian School of Composition is regarded as dating
from the works of Anton König (1836–1911) and probably has
had more illustrious exponents than any other so-called school,
including famous composers of several different European
nationalities.

Rather than emphasizing some single striking mainplay or
strategic maneuver, a problemist composing in the Bohemian
manner endeavors to combine several harmoniously balanced
lines of play in which beautiful mating positions are brought
about by the active maneuvering of all the white pieces.
Artistic construction is considered of greater importance than

45

MIROSLAV HAVEL
Bohemia
September 18, 1904

White mates in three moves

46

MIROSLAV HAVEL
Zlata Praha
November 4, 1904

White mates in three moves

47

MIROSLAV HAVEL
Nove Parizke Mody
December 1, 1904

White mates in three moves

48

MIROSLAV HAVEL
Zlata Praha
October 17, 1917

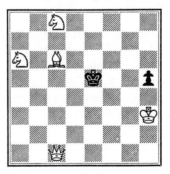

White mates in four moves

purely strategic conceptions. As a definite corollary to this philosophy of composition, echoing lines of play and of mating positions are frequently featured in such works.

Miroslav Kostal (1881–1958), who published his problems under the *nom de plume* of Miroslav Havel, is universally acknowledged to have been the outstanding exponent of the Bohemian type of composition during the first half of the present century. He composed scores of lightweight problems, of which in many instances the major feature was the echo of a model mate, often showing some unusual arrangement of the mating forces.

In No. 45 the promotion of the black pawn to a knight and the move of the king to h2 lead to a pair of chameleon echoed model mates, in the first of which the white queen returns to d6, her initial location (a *switchback*), and in the second plays to one square further, d7, to give mate. No. 46 is another study in black promotions; the promotions of two black pawns, either to queen or knight, leading to four distinct lines of play, two of them ending in echoed pin-model mates, with a third model following 1 – – Pf1 (Q).

In the oddly constructed No. 47 it is a white pawn that promotes to a knight to discover an unusual type of mate. Both lines of play end in model mates. This titbit actually has a "Loydesque" savor. With a waiting-move key, another rather unusual model mate is echoed in No. 48, each of the white knights being sacrificed in turn, followed by mates by the queen along the c-file and along the fifth rank.

Besides a pair of echoed model mates in No. 49, there are two other model mates. The plausible *try*, 1 Qf6, is defeated by 1 – – Ph3. The black king has so much apparent freedom in No. 50 that it may take even an expert solver some time to find a mate in four moves. The play works out with the precision of a geometrical demonstration, showing a fourfold echo of a symmetrical mate.

No. 51 is another miniature in which the white rooks are the protagonists. From the initial position the solver is not likely to suspect that the theme is the promotion of the white pawn to a third rook on two adjacent squares to echo a mate; a striking illustration of the versatility of Havel's genius. Each of the white pieces, except the king, have active roles in the beautiful No. 52, with four continuations ending in model mates.

49

MIROSLAV HAVEL
Zlata Praha
November, 1918

White mates in three moves

50

MIROSLAV HAVEL
Skakbladet
December, 1920

White mates in four moves

51

MIROSLAV HAVEL
American Chess Bulletin
1924

White mates in four moves

52

MIROSLAV HAVEL
First Prize
British Chess Federation
1948

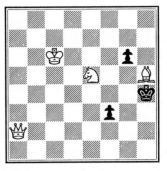

White mates in four moves

Celebrated Collaborators

WITH EDITORS of chess columns, who are also composers, it probably is a fairly common practice to suggest a correction of an unsound position that may have been submitted for publication, or perhaps to make some minor alteration, without regarding the revised version as a joint composition or taking any credit for the amendment.

Then in frequent instances two composers, interested in the same theme, may occasionally collaborate on some individual problem, as Shinkman and Wurzburg did in several instances, fourteen of their joint productions being reproduced in *The Golden Argosy*.

Henry Wald Bettmann (1868–1935) collaborated in his early years with his brother Edgar Bettmann (1866–1945) and his cousin Jacob Bettmann (1865–1915) in the composition of brilliant two-movers. In later years, after becoming prominent in Cincinnati as a physician and surgeon, he continued to compose individually, being especially interested in complex strategic and task compositions.

To a more considerable extent the English composer George Hume (1862–1936) collaborated with other problemists; notably with Duncan Pirnie (1885–1959) and with C. S. Kipping (1891–1964). The 151 problems reproduced in *Changing Fashions*, the 1925 volume of *The Christmas Series* that was devoted to Hume's work, include thirteen joint compositions by Hume and Pirnie, and eleven by Hume and Kipping. Kipping also collaborated with Gerald F. Anderson (b. 1898) as well as with Hume. The majority of the problems by these composers, however, were composed individually.

Similarly Vincent L. Eaton (1915–1962) had the collaboration of Anderson, while Anderson was living in Washington, in the composition of several three-movers involving strategic themes in which they both were interested.

53

JOHANNES KOHTZ and
CARL KOCKELKORN
London Chess Congress
1862

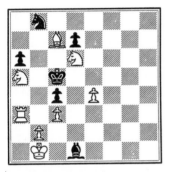

White mates in four moves

54

JOHANNES KOHTZ and
CARL KOCKELKORN
Honorable Mention
Palamede
1865

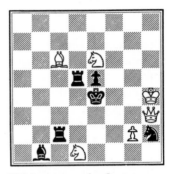

White mates in five moves

55

JOHANNES KOHTZ and
CARL KOCKELKORN
Second Prize
British Tourney
1866

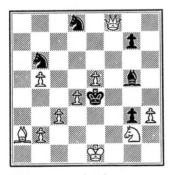

White mates in three moves

56

JOHANNES KOHTZ and
CARL KOCKELKORN
Oesterreichische Schachzeitung
July, 1874

White mates in three moves

The most celebrated composing team in chess problem history was that of the German problemists, Johannes Kohtz (1843–1918) and Carl Kockelkorn (1843–1914) who, throughout half a century, collaborated in the composition of problems notable both for strategic features and their polished presentation. In such collaborative work Kohtz was commonly credited with the origination of the ideas and Kockelkorn with the technique for presenting them artistically. The accompanying problems are examples of the wide range of their talents.

Composed a century ago, with a key threatening an immediate mate, No. 53 seems decidedly *Old School* today, but the complete block following the *en passant* capture by the black pawn and White's third move is an interesting one. Alain White spoke of it as a "curious bottling up feature." 1 – – Pb3 or 1 – – Be2 leads to a mate in three moves, since White continues 2 R × B ck and White's knight's pawn can then advance without being intercepted.

No. 54 has a bizarre theme; the white king making four consecutive moves to clear the rook's file so the queen can mate by 5 Qh7, while the bishop, the only piece Black can move without allowing immediate mate, makes ineffectual moves.

While the keymove of No. 55 is perhaps the first move that a solver would try, White's threatened continuation is not so apparent. The theme of the problem is the three-fold queen sacrifice, differentiated by moves of the black knights, in which connection the anticipatory self-blocking in two of the variations should not be overlooked. Problem No. 56 is another study in queen sacrifices, in which a pawn promotion gives White a second queen; each of them being sacrificed in two variations, with the remaining queen mating—a truly original conception!

No. 57 is a slight affair in which Black threatens a stalemate by playing 1 – – Bh1 and 2 – – Pg2. It is reproduced here because ten years after it was published Loyd used the same device, in a more elaborate four-move problem, which he wagered Steinitz could not solve within the same length of time that it took Loyd to compose it. Steinitz was a keen analyst and after a careful examination of the position he announced that he had solved it, but he had overlooked this threatened

57

JOHANNES KOHTZ and
CARL KOCKELKORN
Schachaufgaben
1875

White mates in five moves

58

JOHANNES KOHTZ and
CARL KOCKELKORN
Brunswick Chess Club
1880

White mates in four moves

59

JOHANNES KOHTZ and
CARL KOCKELKORN
Sonntagsblatt fuer Jedermann
1881

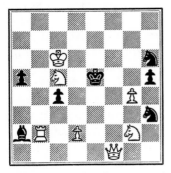

White mates in three moves

60

JOHANNES KOHTZ and
CARL KOCKELKORN
Brentano Tourney
1882

White mates in three moves

stalemating defense. So afterward Loyd referred to it as the "Stuck Steinitz" problem, much to Steinitz' annoyance.

In No. 58 two queen sacrifices, followed by the sacrifice of one rook or its fellow, forces self-blocking by the black knights, permitting the remaining rook to mate. The mates echo each other in a remarkably economical rendering.

A fine key in No. 59 leads to two variations following an *en passant* capture by a black pawn; one of which ends in a mirror model mate, while in the second the capture results in the obstruction of Black's bishop. No. 60 may prove difficult to solve, since the initial position would not suggest to the solver that the theme of the problem is the promotion of a pawn to queen or knight in two unusual mating arrangements, and White's second-move continuations are subtle.

The switchback of the white king in No. 61 is certainly an unusual maneuver. Besides the sparkling mainplay—1 Kf5, S × R ck; 2 Kg5, S × B; 3 Sc7—the capture of the bishop by 1 – – S × B is met by a quiet waiting-move. In an economical rendering, a knight-bishop battery is set up in No. 62 to fire first in one direction and then in another at a right angle to the first.

In No. 63 what is known as the *Roman theme* is doubled. In the initial position if White plays 1 Sf4-e6, threatening mate either by 2 Sc5 or 2 Sf8, the black bishop can defend against both mates by 1 – – Bb4. Similarly if White plays 1 Sd5, threatening mate by 2 Sb6 and also by 2 Sf6, the black rook can defend against both by 1 – – R × P. But White's keymove 1 Qf2, threatening a mate by the queen, forces her to be captured either by the bishop or by the rook. Whichever piece makes the capture, however, is *decoyed* to a square (f2) from which it then cannot play so as to defeat a double mating threat. If 1 – – B × Q; 2 Sf4-e6, Bc5; 3 S × B; or if 1 – – R × Q; 2 Sd5, Rf6; 3 S × R. A further black defense is an additional interesting feature. Should Black play 1 – – Sc6, defending against White's checks, 2 Qa7 ck and 2 Qd4 ck, White continues 2 Qc5, and if Black then checks with the knight either from a7 or d4, White captures the knight with the queen, mating.

In No. 64 the moves of the white queen first decoy the black bishop and then the black rook across the *critical square* e4. Then White plays 3 Qh7, threatening mate by 4 Qb1. If the bishop

61

JOHANNES KOHTZ and
CARL KOCKELKORN
Sonntagsblatt fuer Jedermann
June 11, 1884

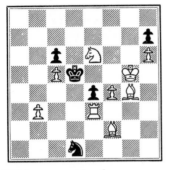

White mates in three moves

62

JOHANNES KOHTZ and
CARL KOCKELKORN
Münchener Neueste Nachrichten
January 13, 1901

White mates in four moves

63

JOHANNES KOHTZ and
CARL KOCKELKORN
V Deutsches Wochenschach
November 11, 1906

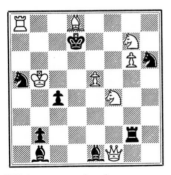

White mates in three moves

64

JOHANNES KOHTZ and
CARL KOCKELKORN
Festschrift des Akad.
Schachklubs, München
1911

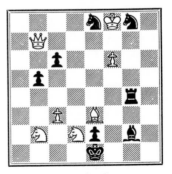

White mates in four moves

moves onto the critical square, 3 – – Be4, to prevent the queen from reaching b1, it interferes with the rook so that White can mate by 4 Qh4. On the other hand if 3 – – Re4, the rook interferes with the bishop and White mates by 4 Qh1. This type of mutual interference between a black rook and a bishop is termed a *Grimshaw interference*, since it is believed to have been first shown in a problem by Walter Grimshaw (1832–1890), published in the *Illustrated London News*, August 24, 1850. A quadrupling of Grimshaw interferences is shown in Loyd's "Organ Pipes" problem, No. 9.

A Consummate Artist

GODFREY HEATHCOTE (1870–1952) was unquestionably England's greatest composer. Not so prolific as many other problemists, none of his work was mediocre; he always was the
consummate artist. Although not a specialist in the composition
of two-movers—like Gamage, Ellerman, Mansfield, Guidelli
or Schiffmann—he composed two-movers that are classic
examples of their themes. He also composed notable three-
movers, but it was in the four-move field that his genius was
recognized as pre-eminent.

No. 65 is an illustration of the *Nowotny interference*, explained
in *The Good Companion Two-Mover*, page 119: "The favorite
form, or perhaps one should say the simplest form, of black
interference has been the mutual obstruction of the Rook and
the Bishop. This was dubbed Nowotny interference by J.
Kohtz, when a white piece is sacrificed on the square of mutual
interference, and Grimshaw interference, when the interference occurs without white sacrifice on the square of interference. The names were given after the composers supposed
by Kohtz to be the pioneers, though the Nowotny dates back
to Brede, Turton and Kempe prior to Nowotny's more celebrated example. The name, however, is generally understood
and should be retained." The problem by Anton Nowotny
(1829–1871) supposed by Kohtz to be the pioneer example of
the interference was published in the *Leipziger Illustrirte Zeitung*,
April 29, 1854. Ordinarily in a Nowotny interference there is
a double mating threat, for when a white man moves onto the
square where the lines of movement of a black rook and bishop
intersect, mates are threatened on two squares, one having
been guarded by the rook and one by the bishop. Whichever
black piece captures the white man interferes with its fellow,
allowing White to mate. In No. 65, however, no such dual
mates are threatened, since the keymove affords the black king

37

a flight square and sets up a new threat. But the capture of the keypiece by the rook or the bishop not only interferes with the guard of its fellow but also results in a self-block, permitting White to mate. Illustrations of Grimshaw interferences have already been shown in problems No. 9 and No. 64.

Were it Black's move in the initial position of No. 66, 1 – – Pe1(Q) would lead to a mate by 2 Qg2 and 1 – – Pe1(S) to mate by 2 Qf2. This set play is changed by the key, but the three cross-checking variations are not changed. To the author this is a memorable problem, since it was the first prize-winner in the first tourney in which the author won recognition; two of his entries being awarded the second and fourth prizes respectively, in a contest in which most of the leading two-move composers of that time competed.

No. 67 may be regarded as a task problem, being an example of what is known as a *black knight wheel*. Any of the eight possible moves of the knight, vacating the d4 square and so defeating the threat, leads to a different mate, and in none of the variations is the knight captured, which is considered a desirable feature. This is a classic illustration of the theme.

With its *flight-sacrifice* keymove, No. 68 is undoubtedly one of the most brilliant block-threat two-movers ever composed. In the initial position a mate is "set" for any move that Black may make; in other words Black is "blocked,"—in a player's language Black is in a *zugzwang*—but White has no available waiting move and so is obliged to make a threat. Hence this type of problem is called a *block-threat*.

With a spectacular withdrawal key, No. 69, a miniature, echoes a model mate in the play following the threat and after 1 – – Ke5. There is also a third model: 1 Bh7, Kd4; 2 Qd2 ck, Ke5; 3 Sg4. The tourney in which No. 70 was entered was restricted to problems with twelve or fewer men. The key yields two flight squares and a queen sacrifice on one of the second moves leads to echoed model mates. In No. 71, one of Heathcote's favorite "no queen" problems, there are six second-move continuations, only one of which is a checking move. With another excellent withdrawal key, there is a model mate in the threat line in No. 72, and also in three of the variations, three of the mates being mirrors.

While other English problemists composed some beautiful

65

GODFREY HEATHCOTE
First Prize
English Mechanic
1891

White mates in two moves

66

GODFREY HEATHCOTE
First Prize
Révue d'Echecs
1904

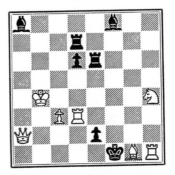

White mates in two moves

67

GODFREY HEATHCOTE
First Prize
Hampstead and Highgate
Express
1905–1906

White mates in two moves

68

GODFREY HEATHCOTE
First Prize
Block-threat Tourney
American Chess Bulletin
1911–1912

White mates in two moves

four-movers, Heathcote's work in the four-move field was outstanding. The strategy in several of his four-move master-pieces, as shown in the accompanying problems, was based on sacrifices of the queen to bring about the desired mating finale, frequently by forcing Black to self-block his king.

With a remarkable economy of the white force, an excellent key in No. 73 is followed by five sacrifices of the queen, according to Black's play, four of the continuations ending in model mates, two of them being echoes. In No. 74 queen sacrifices, in the threat line and also in three of the variations, force self-blocking by one or the other black knight, and three of the lines end in model mates.

In *The Chess Problem* Weenink commented on No. 75 at length: "the theme is the presentation of a series of model mates by the Pf2 introduced by sacrifices of the white Queen. In each mate the guard of the King's field consists of four squares covered by the White rook, three by the two bishops, and one by the white Pawn (or, after 1 − − S × P; 2 − − B × Q, by the block of the black Pawn). These mates are practically all echoes of one another, the white Rook being guarded by one of the Bishops after the three lines: 1 − − Pf5; 2 − − K × Q; 1 − − Ke4; 2 − − B × Q; and 1 − − S × P; 2 − − B × Q. Only in the last, as just noted, is a black Pawn block substituted for the white Pawn guard. In the fourth line, 1 − − B × Q; 2 − − Ke5, the white Rook is guarded by a white Pawn, the Bishop assuming guard of another corner square. The first two lines indicated form a perfect chameleon echo. . . . The third line would be considered as a third echo by all but the most fastidious; while the fourth line terminates in a mate closely analogous, if not actually an echo. The task influence, discussed so fully in dealing with the English two-mover, is here clearly seen, as a four-fold set of Pawn mates with all echo mates would constitute an amazing task record. But the artistic influence is present in that the mates are not absolutely perfect echoes throughout. The distinction is small, but sufficient to raise the problem above task monotony. Then the strategic interest of the Queen sacrifices in every main line of play gives the position a vigour no ordinary task could claim."

In reproducing No. 76 in the March-April, 1941, issue of the *American Chess Bulletin*, of which the author was then the

69

GODFREY HEATHCOTE
Honorable Mention
English Mechanic
1890

White mates in three moves

70

GODFREY HEATHCOTE
First Prize
British Chess Magazine
1904–1906

White mates in three moves

71

GODFREY HEATHCOTE
V Lasker's Chess Magazine
1905–1908 Tourney
(Reading Observer,
January 1, 1910)

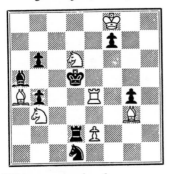

White mates in three moves

72

GODFREY HEATHCOTE
First Prize
Natal Mercury
1914–1916

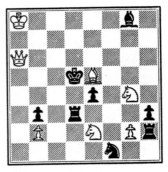

White mates in three moves

73

GODFREY HEATHCOTE
First Prize
Westminster Gazette
1914

White mates in four moves

74

GODFREY HEATHCOTE
First Prize
Falkirk Herald
1914–1915

White mates in four moves

75

GODFREY HEATHCOTE
First Prize
Westminster Gazette
1921

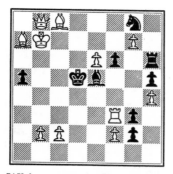

White mates in four moves

76

GODFREY HEATHCOTE
First Prize
Charles Planck Memorial
Tourney
British Chess Federation
1940

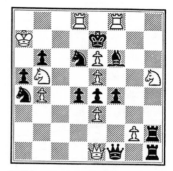

White mates in five moves

editor of the Problem Department, he wrote "Composed in the 'Grand Manner' 3155 is a monumental masterpiece. Any one who works out the solution in detail may well be proud of his solving ability. There are four full length lines ending in model mates, and numerous secondary variations. Three of the model mates are given by pawns; two of them being symmetrical echoes."

A Great Problem Patron

ALAIN WHITE (1880–1951), who had a remarkably wide range of social, philanthropic and literary interests, unquestionably did more for the advancement of the chess problem art than any other individual.

As he relates in *Memories of my Chess Board*, which he published in 1909, he could not "remember the day when I did not know at least the moves of chess." His father, John Jay White, was a keen solver and with his encouragement Alain, when only eleven, had already developed some solving skill. He soon tried his hand at composition and his first attempt was published in the *Dubuque Chess Journal* in December, 1891. Then through his father he became acquainted with Sam Loyd, who began to send problems to Alain to test. "He was the first composer I knew; he remains the greatest I have ever known." Their friendship continued until Loyd's death in 1911.

He became a talented composer, as shown in the accompanying problems. The majority of his problems were two-movers, and he was especially interested in task composition and the illustration of unusual maneuvers. His many other activities in the problem field, however, overshadowed his composing skill.

In 1902 he had written to Arthur Ford Mackenzie, the famous composer living in Jamaica, "offering to continue the collection previously published in his *Chess: Its Poetry and its Prose* in a second volume to bring his compositions up-to-date." This resulted in the publication in 1905 of the 476-page *Chess Lyrics*, which did not appear, however, until shortly after Mackenzie's death. Quoting further from White's *Memories*: "In one sense only the publication of 'Chess Lyrics' was a failure. . . . Its sale was satisfactory, as far as the sale of a chess book ever is; but I realized that invalids and owners of few books did not buy it. They could not afford it. Yet they were the ones I wanted to reach."

This realization led White to consider the preparation, printing and distribution of a series of less elaborate volumes at his own expense. The result was the birth of *The Christmas Series*, which came to be so named because White sent out the books at the Christmas season to composers and problem enthusiasts all over the world.

Beginning in 1905 with *Roi acculé aux angles*, the series was continued annually to 1936, the final volume being a selection of Comins Mansfield's problems entitled *A Genius of the Two-Mover*. Several times two books were issued during a year, so that the series actually included forty-four books, counting *Chess Lyrics* as the first. While the earlier books were edited by White himself, for most of the later volumes he had the collaboration of other composers, notably that of George Hume, whose name appears in connection with nearly half of the titles of the series.

In 1910 White contributed a series of articles to the *British Chess Magazine*, which were studies of problemistic themes, and in 1911 he published them in a paperbound volume, *First Steps in the Classification of Two-Movers*. For this work he had already begun to compile a collection of problems, and he encouraged other problem students to assist him, so that soon he was receiving contributions from correspondents from all quarters of the globe. Not only did the collection begin to become invaluable in suggesting lines for composers to explore, but also for enabling tourney judges to ascertain more readily whether or not a tourney entry might have been anticipated by some earlier problem.

The collection continued to grow until by 1926 it included over two hundred thousand problems. Then, because of his many interests outside of chess, White no longer felt in a position to handle the work and so turned over all of the material to George Hume, to be housed in Hume's home in Nottingham, England. Hume acted as curator until his death in 1936, when the collection was placed in charge of the British Chess Problem Society, under the general supervision of C. S. Kipping. Ultimately it was divided into many distinct sections, each with an individual curator.

Years later White interested Frank Altschul in issuing a series of beautifully printed problem books from his private

Overbrook Press, in Stamford, Connecticut, that began with *A Century of Two-Movers*, and which were either edited by White or with his cooperation.

As the author has previously emphasized, one of Alain White's greatest contributions to the chess problem art lay in his remarkable ability to enlist the enthusiastic collaboration of so many persons throughout the world, with whom he maintained a voluminous correspondence. In the author's personal experience this correspondence covered a period of nearly half a century, during which White also read the manuscripts of two of the author's works—*The Enjoyment of Chess Problems* and *The American Two-Move Chess Problem*—and made numerous constructive suggestions. Although meeting Alain White on only a couple of occasions, the author always considered him as one of his personal friends.

In the initial position of No. 77 the white king is threatened with a double-check by 1 – – P × P ck. The keymove permits Black to give two other double-checks. No. 78 is a waiting-move problem in which six mates are set; the odd keymove adds another mate. The keymove of No. 79, also a waiting-move problem, transfers the pinning of the white knight on d3 from one black rook to its fellow and changes some of the mating play.

No. 80 is still another waiting-move composition, being what is termed an *incomplete block*, because no mate is arranged to meet moves of the black bishop. The variation 1 Rb4, Qd4; 2 Rb3 is particularly interesting, for although the black queen unpins the white bishop it also obstructs the rook's guard on e4, which now must be retained by the bishop; but by interfering with the black bishop's guard on b3, the rook can move to that square to mate.

The key in No. 81 is excellent, since from the initial position the solver would naturally be led to believe that the set rook-bishop battery was designed to function in some of the mates and so might be loath to abandon it. The problem is an example of a complete black knight wheel, which is also shown in Heathcote's No. 67 and Beers' No. 92.

In No. 82 the key permits the white king to be checked with three different cross-checks, depending upon to which square the black knight moves. Cross-checks are combined with

77

ALAIN WHITE
V Cricket and Football Field
April 21, 1906

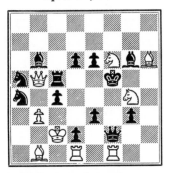

White mates in two moves

78

ALAIN WHITE
The Westminster Gazette
1917

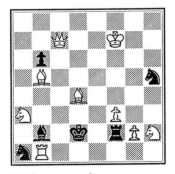

White mates in two moves

79

ALAIN WHITE
Second Prize
First Complete Block Tourney
Good Companions
April, 1918

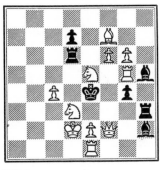

White mates in two moves

80

ALAIN WHITE
First Prize
Seventh Meredith Tourney
Good Companions
May, 1918

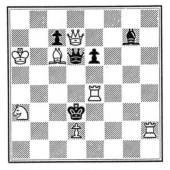

White mates in two moves

81

ALAIN WHITE
The Canadian Courier
1918

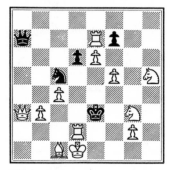

White mates in two moves

82

ALAIN WHITE
Good Companions
May, 1918

White mates in two moves

83

ALAIN WHITE
Good Companions
March, 1920

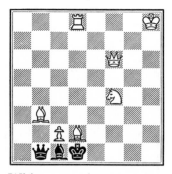

White mates in two moves

84

ALAIN WHITE
American Chess Bulletin
January-February, 1942

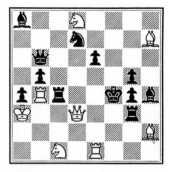

White mates in two moves

half-pinning in an economical rendering in No. 83. The term *half-pin* is applied to the arrangement where two black men are on a line between the black king and a long-range white piece. While neither black man is initially pinned, if either moves off the line its fellow becomes pinned.

A *line-pinned* piece is one that can move along the line on which it is pinned, but cannot move off it. No. 84 features the play between a line-pinned white queen and a line-pinned black rook, in which the major thematic variation is 1 Qc3, Rd4; 2 Qe3. Further examples of Alain White's composing skill are shown in problems 117 and 123.

A Happy Hobby

THE COMPOSITION and solving of chess problems has proved a godsend to many who because of physical disabilities have been unable to enjoy more active avocations. As Alain White stated, he had many such individuals in mind when he decided to embark on the publishing of his *Christmas Series*. Among composers who labored under physical, or other handicaps, Meredith, Mackenzie, Kuskop, Marble, Kish and Beers were especially prominent.

William Meredith (1835–1903), after being admitted to the bar in Philadelphia, was obliged to retire in a few years because of ill health and remained an invalid until his death at sixty-eight. He began problem composition in 1870 and continued to compose at intervals throughout the remainder of his life.

His earlier problems were contributed to Brownson's *Dubuque Chess Journal*, in which about three-quarters of his compositions eventually were published, his total output being less than two hundred problems. Although his work did not attain any wide recognition before his death, with the reawakening of interest in problems in Philadelphia brought about by the formation of the Good Companion Chess Problem Club in 1913, his talents became more generally appreciated. Because of the economical construction of so many of his problems, two-movers with a total of twelve or fewer men came to be termed "Merediths" and the Good Companion Club held tourneys especially for such compositions.

One hundred of Meredith's problems were reproduced in the 1916 volume of *The Christmas Series*, with individual comments on them by members of the Club.

In this book Otto Wurzburg commented on No. 85: "A remarkable block problem with two added mates, one of them, after 1 – – K × S, the finest in the problem. The key is a wonderfully fine and difficult one."

Charles Promislo calls No. 86 "probably Meredith's most widely known two-mover. . . . The splendid key, with a threat that seems easily parried, is of the highest order."

For over two decades from the eighteen-eighties Arthur Ford Mackenzie (1861–1905) was one of the brightest stars in the chess problem firmament. Both in two-move and three-move tourneys he won prize after prize; over a hundred of them being listed in the Introduction to *Chess Lyrics*.

Quoting Alain White from that introduction: "Perhaps the keynote of Mr. Mackenzie's genius may be defined as his Cosmopolitanism. He has assimilated more than any other composer the best traits of each of the principal schools of construction without following any of them slavishly. Thus, speaking in a general manner, he is fond of the striking moves which are so dear to American composers, and he presents his chief ideas with the beauty and precision of Continental standards, paying at the same time the close attention to accuracy in minor details which is associated with English problems."

His eyesight gradually failing, at the age of thirty-five Mackenzie became totally blind in February, 1896; yet paradoxically he did some of his finest work in his later years.

Incidentally this has led the author to become interested in endeavoring to learn how most problemists compose. If a person is a fair visualizer, blindness may not prove too great a handicap to composition. In playing the game, the player in deciding upon a move cannot touch the men, but must visualize various possible continuations. Then, of course, there are many expert "blindfold" players.

In the author's own composing he seldom has used board and men, except occasionally to test a problem for soundness, but first has visualized an idea in his "mind's eye" and then made a rough penciled diagram on which he could make erasures as he progressed in the development of his composition. In talking with the author about his method of composing, Walter I. Kennard (1860–1936) said that he composed in practically the same way, because when he had once set up a position on a board his ideas seemed "to freeze" and he found it difficult to improve the position further. Sam Loyd apparently did much of his composing in a somewhat similar fashion, of which his "Steinitz Gambit" was a typical example.

No. 87 was Mackenzie's favorite three-mover, which he felt earned the most important honor of his composing career. In making his award in the Tenth Tourney of the *Sydney Morning Herald*, the judge, J. J. Glynn, stated that No. 88 "is the finest two-mover of my experience."

Friedrich A. L. Kuskop (1844–1938), who was born in Germany and then went to live in Wellington, New Zealand, was another problemist who continued to compose after he became blind. The Meredith, No. 89, with two flight squares for the black king, thematic key and two sparkling cross-checking variations, is an excellent example of his composing ability. He also won the second prize in the Second Meredith Tourney of the Good Companions, held in 1916. Another of his prize-winning Merediths is problem No. 146.

Murray Marble (1885–1919), a life-long invalid, composed some three hundred problems, his most notable tourney success being the winning of the first prize in both the two-move and the three-move sections of the *La Stratégie* tourney in 1909, held in memory of its former editor, Numa Preti (1841–1908). The term *half-pin* originated in some correspondence between Marble and Comins Mansfield in 1913, although a half-pin had been shown as early as 1859 in a problem by William Greenwood (1836–1922). The brilliant, flight-yielding key in No. 90 submits the bishop to capture by any one of seven black men.

Alexander Kish, an inmate for some years in an institution for the criminal insane, died in 1937. Originally a strong player, he became interested in problem composition in 1930 and developed into a brilliant technician. But since he lacked the contacts necessary to learn what other composers had already done, some of his complex compositions proved to have been anticipated, as shown by problems 149 and 150 in this volume. He corresponded with the author, who placed many of his problems in both American and English chess columns.

No. 91 is an example of the *Schiffmann Defense*, named after the renowned Rumanian composer, J. A. Schiffmann (1904–1930). In this theme White threatens mate by discovery from a battery, to avert which Black self-pins a man in such a way that if White still endeavors to carry out the threat, the firing piece of the battery will then unpin the self-pinned black man

85

WILLIAM MEREDITH
Dubuque Chess Journal
December, 1886

White mates in two moves

86

WILLIAM MEREDITH
First Prize
Ninth Tourney
Dubuque Chess Journal
December, 1889

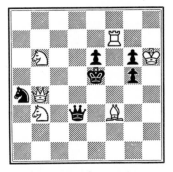

White mates in two moves

87

ARTHUR F. MACKENZIE
First Prize
Eleventh Tourney
British Chess Magazine
1902

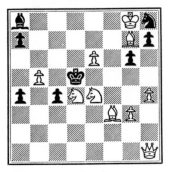

White mates in three moves

88

ARTHUR F. MACKENZIE
First Prize
Tenth Tourney
Sydney Morning Herald
1904–1905

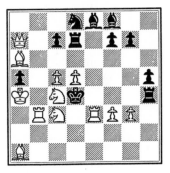

White mates in two moves

89

FRIEDRICH A. L. KUSKOP
Second Prize
First Meredith Tourney
Good Companions
May, 1915

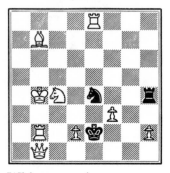

White mates in two moves

90

MURRAY MARBLE
First Prize
La Stratégie
1908–1909

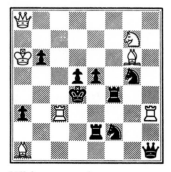

White mates in two moves

91

ALEXANDER KISH
American Chess Bulletin
January, 1936

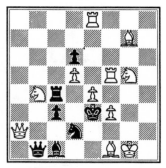

White mates in two moves

92

WILLIAM A. BEERS
Atlanta Journal
September 14, 1934

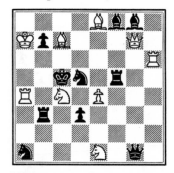

White mates in two moves

and allow it to interpose to prevent the mate. Kish triples this theme in No. 91, where Black's self-pinning defenses are the capture of the white pawn on e4 by the queen, rook or knight.

William Beers, another life-long invalid, lived in an institution at Willmar, Minnesota, where he died in 1942. One of his thematic two-movers was awarded the first prize in the informal tourney for 1939 of the *American Chess Bulletin*. In the black knight wheel of No. 92 the knight makes seven interferences on other black pieces and is captured only in the eighth variation.

An Intriguing Theme

THE MUTUAL INTERFERENCE between two black pieces of like movement—the two rooks, or the queen moving on the same diagonal with a bishop—has interested many composers.

A problem that Walter Grimshaw entered in the London Tourney of 1852 featured the interference of one black rook on another, but the interference was not mutual. Then Loyd, who was the pioneer in illustrating so many themes, showed a mutual interference of the rooks in a prize-winning problem published in November, 1857 (No. 93). Opening with an aggressive key, a quiet second move leads to the strategic variations.

The next year a lighter position, but also with an aggressive key which threatened a short mate, was published by Joseph Plachutta (d. 1883) in the *Leipziger Illustrirte Zeitung* (No. 94). Possibly because Plachutta's problem, being published in Europe, may have attracted more attention than Loyd's earlier rendering of the theme, the mutual interference came to be known as a *Plachutta interference*.

Years later Darso J. Densmore (1867–1917), Loyd's son-in-law and a talented composer, especially of strategic problems, became particularly interested in the Plachutta interference and composed a whole series of problems featuring it, many of which were reproduced in the 1920 volume of *The Christmas Series*, which was *A Memorial to D. J. Densmore*.

In the original version of the theme a white man is sacrificed on the *critical square*, the square on which the moves of the two black pieces intersect; d5 in problem 93 and g7 in problem 94. The theme is essentially a three-move one and the initial moves in Nos. 93 and 94, being unrelated to the theme, would be regarded as objectionable today.

In No. 95 and No. 96, however, the interference is repeated on different critical squares, requiring the full four moves for the

93

SAMUEL LOYD
V First Prize
American Chess Monthly
November, 1857

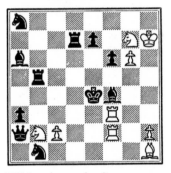

White mates in four moves

94

JOSEPH PLACHUTTA
Leipziger Illustrirte Zeitung
August 28, 1858

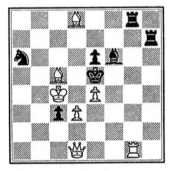

White mates in four moves

95

DARSO J. DENSMORE
V The Pittsburgh Gazette-Times
December 3, 1916

White mates in four moves

96

DARSO J. DENSMORE
The Pittsburgh Gazette-Times
December 31, 1916

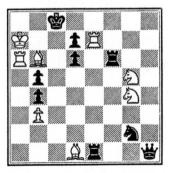

White mates in four moves

97

OTTO WURZBURG
V Zlata Praha
June 25, 1909

White mates in three moves

98

KENNETH S. HOWARD
The Pittsburgh Post
March 29, 1925

White mates in three moves

99

DARSO J. DENSMORE
V Third Prize
The Pittsburgh Gazette-Times
March 19, 1916

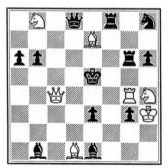

White mates in three moves

100

KENNETH S. HOWARD
V The Western Morning News
and Daily Gazette
July 10, 1937

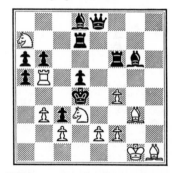

White mates in three moves

101
DARSO J. DENSMORE
The Pittsburgh Gazette-Times
December 3, 1916

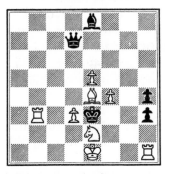

White mates in four moves

102
DARSO J. DENSMORE
The Pittsburgh Gazette-Times
November 26, 1916

White mates in three moves

103
LOUIS H. JOKISCH
First Prize, Class B
The Densmore Memorial
Tourney
1918

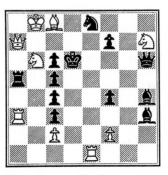

White mates in four moves

104
HENRY WALD BETTMANN
Tasks and Echoes
1915

White mates in three moves

maneuvering. In No. 95 the critical squares are f3 and d3.
No. 96 is a remarkable composition. With the queen operating
as a rook there are nine distinct mutual interferences between
the rooks and the queen and rooks.

Wurzburg's beautifully constructed No. 97, with its well-
hidden second-move threat, was a pioneer problem, showing
that a Plachutta interference could be induced without the
sacrifice of a white man on the critical square. Since its publication problems with mutual interferences without such a
sacrifice have been termed *Wurzburg-Plachuttas*. No. 98 illustrates the theme introduced by the threat of a bishop to make a
trip around the board.

With the black queen operating as a rook, Densmore doubles
the interferences of a Wurzburg-Plachutta in No. 99, the critical
squares being f6 and d6. In No. 100 the interferences are also
doubled with d6 and e6 as the critical squares.

Although the Plachutta theme was initially regarded as a
mutual interference between pieces moving horizontally and
vertically—between rooks or the queen operating as a rook—
it came to be applied to similar mutual interferences on diag-
onals between a bishop and the queen moving along a diagonal.
Densmore's No. 101 is an example of such a bishop and queen
mutual interference doubled, the critical squares being e6 and
f5. No. 102 is a bishop-queen Wurzburg-Plachutta.

In No. 103 Louis H. Jokisch (1851–1938) showed mutual
interferences between the queen and each of the bishops in
turn. Since these interferences occur on squares of different
colors, and the resulting play is along both white and black dia-
gonals, the composition was termed a double *Chameleon Plachutta*.

Dr. Henry Wald Bettmann combined orthogonal and diagonal Wurzburg-Plachuttas in a problem, No. 104, that he
contributed to *Tasks & Echoes*, the 1915 volume of *The Christmas
Series*. Wurzburg's No. 105, in which the black queen operates
both along the file and the diagonal to make a combined orthogonal and diagonal Wurzburg-Plachutta, was also reproduced
in that same volume. The construction of No. 105 is masterly
in that Wurzburg in illustrating the theme employed only five
white pieces.

It was Dr. Bettmann's problem that first aroused the author's
interest in the various possibilities of showing both orthogonal

105
OTTO WURZBURG
V The Pittsburgh Gazette-Times
November 8, 1914

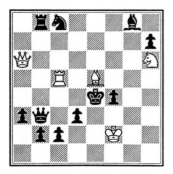

White mates in three moves

106
KENNETH S. HOWARD
V British Chess Magazine
September, 1944

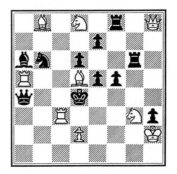

White mates in three moves

107
KENNETH S. HOWARD
The Observer
April 25, 1926

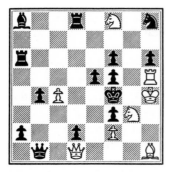

White mates in three moves

108
V. KUKAINIS
Second Prize
Stasti un Romani
1938

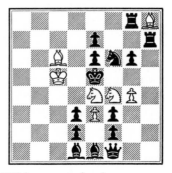

White mates in three moves

and diagonal Plachutta interferences in the same problem and led him to compose a number of such problems in which the strategic play is actuated in several different ways.

In No. 106 Black defends against the threat of 2 Q × Pd5 ck by cutting off the attack of either the queen or the rook on the pawn on d5. The play has a high degree of unity in that the white knights alternate in their roles in the four thematic lines, each making the decoying moves in two variations and the mating moves in two variations.

Other strategic elements are involved in No. 107 besides the Wurzburg-Plachutta interferences. The keymove, 1 Pc5, threatens 2 Pc6, interfering with the lines of guard of both the rook on a6 and the bishop on a8, with the double threat of mate by 3 Sd6 or 3 Q × Pf3, a typical Nowotny interference. A further strategic line is 1 – – Qd3, where the queen interferes with the guard of the rook on the pawn d2. The rook's move to d3 does not lead to a reciprocal line of play, but simply obstructs the queen's guard on the Pf5, permitting 2 R × Pf5, a short mate. Such an interference also occurs in problem No. 100, where 1 – – Qe7 interferes with the bishop's guard on the rook on f6, allowing White to continue 2 B × R ck, Q × B; 3 Pe3.

Where the interference between two black pieces of like motion, instead of being reciprocal, is restricted to the move of one of the pair as in the variations just mentioned, it is known as an *Holzhausen-Plachutta*, named after the composer Baron Walther Freiheer von Holzhausen (1876–1935). Holzhausen discussed in great detail all the various types of interferences in his *Brennpunktprobleme*, a book of 135 pages, of which a second edition was issued in 1926, and which was primarily based on articles he contributed in 1908 and 1909 to the *Deutschen Wochenschach*. In fact in that volume he calls attention to Grimshaw's problem, reproducing it as No. 67. Nevertheless this type of interference is now commonly called a *Holzhausen-Plachutta*, or more usually a *Holzhausen interference*.

The final example of a combined orthogonal and diagonal Wurzburg-Plachutta, No. 108, shows the theme in a waiting-move setting; quite an achievement despite the awkward grouping of the black pawns. As in problem 106, the white knights alternate in making the decoying and mating moves in the four thematic lines.

That Sturdy Fellow—The Rook

ALTHOUGH he never takes a devious course, but always moves in an honest way—straight up or down a file, or along a rank—the sturdy rook may play the leading role in many an interesting maneuver. As the 1910 volume of *The Christmas Series*, Alain White brought out *The White Rooks*, a selection of two hundred and seventy-four problems in which the white forces were restricted to the rooks, plus the king and pawns. This volume aroused so much interest among composers, both in America and Europe, that the next year White issued another volume, *More White Rooks*, containing four hundred positions, over half of which were original compositions contributed specifically for publication in the 1911 book.

While some white rook problems may be simple and easy to solve, others may be relatively complex with more subtle keys and continuations. No. 109 has a good key and pleasing variety, including a surprising sacrifice of one of the rooks. In No. 110 Wolfgang Pauly (1876–1934) shows in a remarkably simple setting how mate can be effected by the promotion of a pawn to a rook, rather than to a queen; actually a stroke of genius! If after the pawn promotes, Black should play 1 – – Ka3, the continuation 2 Rb4 would be a stalemate if the promotion were to a queen, which would guard the a2 square.

By lengthening the solution to four moves, Otto Wurzburg in No. 111 doubles the Bonus Socius theme shown in the first problem of this volume. The black pawn is needed to avoid a dual continuation, since without the pawn after 1 Rh7, Sd4; White could play 2 Rb7, Se6; and then make a waiting move with the king.

In *The White Rooks* Alain White called Loyd's No. 112, in which a knight again is Black's defending piece, "A very brilliant problem, among the half-dozen finest in the collection." A

109

JOHANNES KOHTZ and
CARL KOCKELKORN
*Münchener Neueste
Nachrichten
1892*

White mates in four moves

110

WOLFGANG PAULY
*Deutsche Schachzeitung
February, 1905*

White mates in three moves

111

OTTO WURZBURG
*The Pittsburgh Gazette-Times
February 17, 1918*

White mates in four moves

112

SAMUEL LOYD
*Milwaukee Telegram
circa 1885*

White mates in four moves

113

KENNETH S. HOWARD
American Chess Bulletin
September-October, 1925

White mates in three moves

114

WERNER SPECKMANN
U. S. Problem Bulletin
September-October, 1965

White mates in three moves

115

GODFREY HEATHCOTE
More White Rooks
1911

White mates in four moves

116

KENNETH S. HOWARD
First Honorable Mention
Twelfth Informal Tourney
The Weekly Westminster
January 16, 1925

White mates in four moves

black knight is also the defending piece in No. 113, where the key is not too apparent.

Werner Speckmann's No. 114, featuring a duel between a black rook and the two white ones, has a good key and a couple of quiet continuations. Heathcote's No. 115, contributed as an original problem to *More White Rooks*, has three quiet continuations. All of these first seven problems are miniatures, having only seven or fewer white and black men. Shinkman's No. 33 is also an example of a white rook miniature.

No. 116 is a more elaborate composition, employing ten pawns in addition to the rooks, with four full-length lines of play.

That Peculiar Chap—The Pawn

THE PLEBEIAN PAWN actually has many remarkable characteristics; by perseverance he can change into the most powerful piece on the board; he marches straight forward but can never retreat; nor can he advance if there is any man on the next square ahead. Yet he can be aggressive diagonally, since he can capture any opposing man on an adjacent file that is one rank in advance of the one on which he stands.

On his first move he has the choice of advancing either one or two squares, but afterward he can only move one square at a time. On reaching the eighth rank he cannot remain a so-called "dummy pawn," but by the rules of chess he must burst out of his chrysalis state and become a piece, except that he cannot be promoted to be another king. Problem composers have exploited all the possibilities afforded by these characteristics.

Although in the playing of a game he ordinarily would be promoted to a queen if he succeeds in reaching the eighth rank, problemists have been interested in showing how a so-called "minor" promotion—to a rook, bishop or knight—may be more effective in certain situations. A typical example is Pauly's No. 110 in the preceding chapter.

Another peculiar characteristic of the power of a pawn is that if he is on his fifth rank and a pawn of an opposing color, on an adjacent file, endeavors to bypass him by making a double jump, he can capture it as though it had only moved a single square, such a move being termed an *en passant* capture. This move is frequently featured in problems, and a volume of *The Christmas Series*, entitled *Running the Gauntlet*, also issued in 1911, was devoted to a study of such compositions, with a hundred examples of them.

Standing on his initial square, on the second rank of the board, a white pawn can give four mates, one by a direct capture and three by discovery. This is shown in Alain White's

No. 117 where in the initial position White's king's knight's pawn can give four such mates, differentiated by moves of the black queen, viz., 1 – – Qf3; 2 P × Q; 1 – – Q × S; 2 Pg3; 1 – – Qg5; 2 Pg4: 1 – – Qh3; 2 P × Q. In this brilliant composition, after the keymove 1 Qb1, threatening 2 Qb4, it is the queen's bishop's pawn that delivers four different mates: 1 – – Qd3; 2 P × Q: 1 – – Q × R; 2 Pc3: 1 – – Qe5 or g5; 2 Pc4: 1 – – Qb3; 2 P × Q.

Havel's No. 118, utilizing a pawn's option of advancing either one or two squares on its initial move, shows echoed chameleon model mates, in which the mating positions are exactly duplicated with all the men in the same relative positions one rank lower in the second variation than in the first. From the simple appearance of the problem a solver might not fully realize the remarkable skill required for its composition.

In No. 119 a white pawn, making an *en passant* capture, discovers mate along a diagonal parallel to the one on which it itself is moving. The unpinning of the pawn by the move of the black queen, plus the cross-check, add considerably to the interest of the maneuver.

En passant captures by black pawns also may lead to interesting strategic effects. In two of the lines of Ben Wash's No. 120 the black pawn that makes the *en passant* capture interferes with the movement of the black rook, allowing two thematic mates.

In *Alpine Chess*, the 1921 volume of *The Christmas Series*, No. 121 was reproduced with the comment: "A favorite theme which was fully exploited afterwards. W. Henneberger was not only the pioneer of this theme, for he was able to give it the best expression. Composed in his younger days practically as a joke, it became a gem of the problem art." The next position, No. 122, has *en passant* pawn captures by both black and white in two lines of play.

In the mainplay of Alain White's No. 123, an *en passant* capture by a white pawn opens lines for five white pieces simultaneously—that of both rooks, both bishops and the queen—a task achievement. The secondary play also is interesting, viz., 1 – – Kf6; 2 Qg7 ck, K × Q; 3 Rg4 and 1 – – Bg5; 2 Re4 ck, Kd6; 3 Be5. Pauly's No. 124 shows an idea difficult to illustrate; a black pawn by making an *en passant* capture

117
ALAIN WHITE
American Chess Bulletin
November-December, 1941

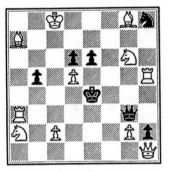

White mates in two moves

118
MIROSLAV HAVEL
Schweizerische Schachzeitung
March, 1918

White mates in five moves

119
KENNETH S. HOWARD
American Chess Bulletin
July-August, 1938

White mates in three moves

120
BENJAMIN S. WASH
Honorable Mention
Huddersfield College Magazine
Tourney
1879–1880

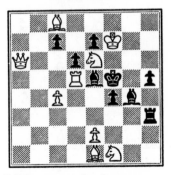

White mates in three moves

121

W. HENNEBERGER
Basler Zeitung
February 13, 1905

White mates in three moves

122

KENNETH S. HOWARD
American Chess Bulletin
May-June, 1938

White mates in three moves

123

ALAIN WHITE
American Chess Weekly
1902

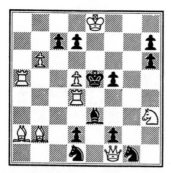

White mates in three moves

124

WOLFGANG PAULY
Running the Gauntlet
1911

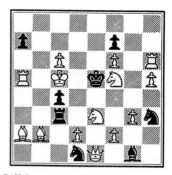

White mates in three moves

125

SAMUEL LOYD
Holyoke Transcript
1877

White mates in three moves

126

WILLIAM A. SHINKMAN
The Chess Amateur
December, 1910

White mates in three moves

127

OTTO WURZBURG
(after Niels Hoeg)
The Pittsburgh Gazette-Times
January 4, 1914

White mates in three moves

128

HENRY WALD BETTMANN
First Prize
Babson Task Contest
1926

White selfmates in three moves

gives double-check to the white king, which in turn discovers mate.

The maneuver in No. 125 is a typical "Loydesque trick"; a pawn promotes to the apparently most ineffective piece, at a maximum distance from the black king.

Shinkman took a great interest in studying the various strategic possibilities of pawn promotions, examples of which have already been shown in problems No. 29 and No. 30. In No. 126 White must "lose a move" in order to mate in three moves and, despite the seemingly open nature of the position, the only possible waiting move is to promote the bishop's pawn to a bishop, which takes no part in the ensuing mating play. The importance of the pawn on g2 should be noted. It prevents the rook from making a waiting move by retreating to the second or first rank and it cannot move without obstructing the rook's subsequent play.

In No. 127 a pawn promotes to each of four different white pieces according to Black's play. A most economical rendering of this task, No. 128, is a famous masterpiece. To counter any black pawn promotions on g1, the pawn on f7 is promoted to the same kind of piece—queen, rook, bishop or knight—all the promotions taking place on the same squares; an astounding achievement, which it would be practically impossible to show in a direct-mate setting.

Twin Problems

WHEN TWO PROBLEMS are nearly identical in their setting, but have some slight difference that changes the solution, they are termed *twins*.

The difference may be in the location of a single man, like that of the white knight in problems No. 129 and No. 130. In each of these the keymove sets up an *indirect masked battery*—one aimed at a square *adjacent* to the one on which the black king stands. In No. 129 the bishop plays to g4 masking the rook and becomes the *firing piece* of the battery when the black king, or the knight on d8, moves. In No. 130, on the other hand, the rook plays to g4 masking the bishop and becomes the firing piece.

The next pair of twins illustrates a change from a *complete block* waiting-move position to a *block-threat* problem, made possible by replacing the black knight on e8 with a black pawn on e7 to guard e6. In No. 131 the knight on e8 prevents the black queen playing to that square after the key, 1 Bc7, a pure waiting move. In No. 132, 1 – – Qe8, by retaining the guard on c6, defeats 1 Bc7. White, however, can now mate in two moves by 1 Qa1, threatening 2 Pc4. In problem 131 Black could make this threat ineffective by playing 1 – – Sd5.

Twin problems sometimes may be formed by a change in the entire location of the men, without any change in the men themselves or in their relation to each other. Nos. 133 and 134 are a famous example. The English composer, Benjamin C. Laws (1861–1931), showed how the solution to problem 133, by the American composer Louis H. Jokisch (1851–1938), could be completely changed by moving all the men one file to the left.

Most twinning problems have appeared only occasionally, incidentally as it were, but Wolfgang Pauly, (1876-1934) the great Rumanian problemist, made a study of their possibilities and

129

F. AUREL TAUBER
Magyar Sakkvilage
October, 1922

White mates in two moves

130

F. AUREL TAUBER
Magyar Sakkvilage
October, 1922

White mates in two moves

131

KENNETH S. HOWARD
American Chess Bulletin
July-August, 1925

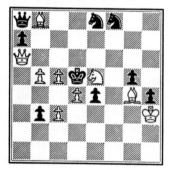

White mates in two moves

132

KENNETH S. HOWARD
American Chess Bulletin
July-August, 1925

White mates in two moves

133

Louis H. Jokisch
Nashville American
March, 1888

White mates in three moves

134

Benjamin G. Laws
(*after Louis H. Jokisch*)
Nashville American
July, 1888

White mates in three moves

135

Wolfgang Pauly
V Neue Wiener Schachzeitung
April, 1923

White mates in four moves

136

Wolfgang Pauly
V Neue Wiener Schachzeitung
April, 1923

White mates in four moves

137

WOLFGANG PAULY
Deutsche Schachzeitung
December, 1906

White mates in four moves

138

WOLFGANG PAULY
Deutsche Schachzeitung
December, 1906

White mates in four moves

139

WOLFGANG PAULY
Deutsche Schachzeitung
January, 1907

White mates in four moves

140

WOLFGANG PAULY
Deutsches Wochenschach
April 7, 1907

White mates in four moves

composed sparkling examples, many of which were reproduced in a selection of Pauly's problems that Dr. M. Niemeijer (b. 1902) published in 1948 under the title *Zo Sprak Wolfgang Pauly*. Pauly's Nos. 135 and 136 show, similarly to Nos. 133 and 134, how the movement of an entire position one file either way, without altering the relation of the men, may change the solution.

The next four problems are not precise illustrations of twinning, since the initial positions of the men vary too much, but the fact that exactly the same pieces are employed in each problem, with the same general relation to the location of the black king, closely relates this fascinating foursome to the preceding compositions.

Coincidences and Anticipations

WHEN SIMILAR PROBLEMS appear practically simultaneously it is termed a *coincidence*. Should a problem be found to duplicate one published some time previously it is said to have been *anticipated*. Since hundreds of problems are published every year it is not surprising to find that occasionally some position duplicates the earlier work of another composer. Coincidences and anticipations are most likely to occur in light-weight problems or in those illustrating some especially clear-cut theme, even where the setting may be complex.

Since increasing attention is being given to making collections of problems classified according to themes, positions now can be more readily checked for anticipations than was possible heretofore. This is of particular importance to judges in making tourney awards, where an entry is disqualified if it is found to have been closely anticipated.

One of the most noted coincidences of former years was the Shinkman-Carpenter coincidence shown in problems 141 and 142, both of which were published in October, 1877. This attracted much attention at the time, since the likelihood of such duplication was not so clearly recognized then as it has been since. The only difference between the two problems is that Carpenter used an unnecessary pawn, at e7, in No. 142.

The Shinkman-Loyd coincidence, Nos. 143 and 144, was especially striking as both problems were entries in the same tourney.

No. 145 and No. 146 are examples of a coincidence where the illustration of a particular theme practically leads to a specific construction. Here the theme is to show three self-blocking moves by the black queen, and the problems were entries in separate tourneys being held at the same time. A minor difference between the problems is that Kuskop employed a white queen where Heathcote used a rook and bishop. This, however,

141

WILLIAM A. SHINKMAN
First Prize
Huddersfield College Magazine
October, 1877

White mates in two moves

142

GEORGE E. CARPENTER
Detroit Free Press
October 20, 1877

White mates in two moves

143

WILLIAM A. SHINKMAN
Centennial Tourney
1876–1877

White mates in three moves

144

SAMUEL LOYD
Centennial Tourney
1876–1877

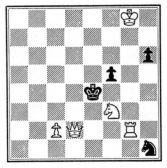

White mates in three moves

145

GODFREY HEATHCOTE
Second Prize
Leisure Hour
1899–1900

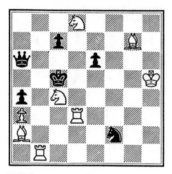

White mates in two moves

146

FRIEDRICH A. L. KUSKOP
First Prize
Canterbury Times
1899–1900

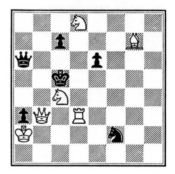

White mates in two moves

147

OTTO WURZBURG
American Chess Bulletin
July–August, 1941

White mates in three moves

148

G. THOREN
Schachwarlden
1929

White mates in three moves

149

ALEXANDER KISH
The Observer
March 14, 1937

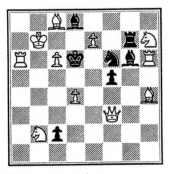

White mates in two moves

150

ARNALDO ELLERMAN
Good Companions
1923

White mates in two moves

151

L. J. LOSCHINSKY
First Prize
Smena
1932

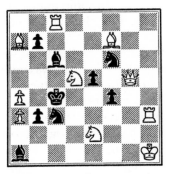

White mates in two moves

152

P. TEN CATE
L'Alfiere di Re
1923

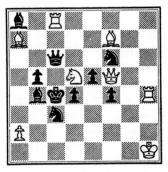

White mates in two moves

resulted in a dual mate in Kuskop's rendering, since after 1 − − Qb6, White can mate by 2 Qc3 or by 2 Qc4.

No. 147 and No. 148 illustrate the likelihood of anticipation in the case of lightweight settings. Wurzburg's No. 147 was reproduced as a frontispiece for the second volume of *A Sketchbook of American Chess Problematists*, published in 1942, and it was several years later that Thoren's earlier problem was brought to the author's attention. Wurzburg's version, with its excellent key, is a trifle superior, but he certainly never would have submitted it for publication in the *American Chess Bulletin* had he seen the earlier problem.

No. 149 is an even more striking example than were problems No. 145 and No. 146 of how the most satisfactory setting for a complex theme may determine the construction of a problem. As previously mentioned Alexander Kish had little opportunity to learn of the work of other composers, and so his almost man-for-man duplication of a problem, No. 150, by the famous South American composer is the more remarkable.

No. 151 and No. 152 are another pair where a complex theme—a quadruple unpinning of a white knight—led to the composing of the similar positions, published nine years apart. The keys are mediocre, since the key pieces are obviously out of play initially; but after the keymoves the queen and king's rook occupy identical squares in both problems. The notable point, however, is that the pair is another example of the fact that a complex theme frequently determines to a large degree the construction required to illustrate it. Despite minor differences in the settings, the play in the four thematic lines of both problems is identical.

Finally No. 153 is an example of where an earlier work was duplicated in every detail. Some time after No. 153 was published the author noticed that J. Hartong had shown the same bishop and knight interferences on a rook in a similar setting, but employing only twelve men, in a problem in the October, 1919, *Good Companion Folder*, which, however, had a flight-taking key. Then long afterward Hertmann's problem, No. 154, with its identical setting with No. 153, was brought to his attention.

In this connection the reader may be interested to learn how two composers may have happened to arrive at identical settings. The author's germ idea in composing No. 153 was to show how

153

KENNETH S. HOWARD
The Western Morning News
April 18, 1936

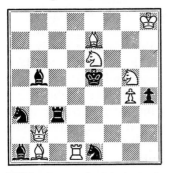

White mates in two moves

154

SÁNDOR HERTMANN
Nationaltidende
1925

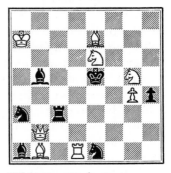

White mates in two moves

155

J. HARTONG
Good Companions
October, 1919

White mates in two moves

interferences by a black bishop on a rook, pinned by the white queen, would permit the queen to unpin the rook in making mating moves. The next step was to provide a mating threat to which such interference moves by the black bishop would be defenses. So he placed the black king in the middle of the board at e5 and planned to have the threatened mate 2 Rd5, which 1 – – Bc4 or Bc6 and 1 – – Bd3 would avert.

Then he saw that the black knights could be employed to make additional interferences on the rook. A knight posted on the a3 square not only could make a third interference but also would guard the bishop on b6. Then the other knight placed on e1 would provide a fourth interference and another thematic variation. To prevent an immediate mate by Q × R, the placing of a black bishop on a1 was plainly indicated. To support the rook when it played to d5 in the threat it was apparent that a bishop could be used most effectively and by locating it initially on the b1 square a good key was available.

Now all that remained to do was to guard the squares in the black king's field, for which the white knights, the other bishop and a pawn provided the necessary force. A black pawn was added at h4 to prevent a second solution by 1 Qh2 ck. The use of the white king was not required, and as it has been the author's practice to leave the king on his own side of the board if not needed elsewhere, he placed him on the h file, as far removed as possible.

Possibly Hertmann had seen Hartong's problem, No. 155, and decided to show the interferences on the rook with a better key, or perhaps the idea merely occurred to him as it did to the author and so he followed a similar procedure in composing No. 154. In any case the credit for the most economical, and for the "classic," rendering of the theme belongs to Hartong and to Hertmann respectively.

Solutions

No. 1
1 Rh7–g7, Sb7; 2 Ra8
          Sf7; 2 Rg8

No. 2
1 Q e1, Pd2 × Q (Q); 2 Rd4 *threat* 3 Ra4 ck, B × R;
                              4 Pb4 ck Q × P; 5 P × Q

No. 3
1 Bc1, Pb4; 2 waiting move, Pb5; 3 Rd2, Kf4; 4 Rd4

No. 4
1 Rh1, Bd7, e8; 2 Q b1, Bb5; 3 Q g1

No. 5
1 Q g1 *threat* 2 Bf2 *threat* 3 B × P *threat* 4 Q c5
                  Kd5; 3 B × P, K × P; 4 Q d4
                        else; 4 Q c5

No. 6
1 S g4 ck, Kh1; 2 Q h2 ck, P × Q; 3 Sf2
           Kh3; 2 Sh2, Pg2; 3 Q h8
                   Kh4; 3 Q h8
                   Pf3; 3 Rh8
       Kf3; 2 Q c2, Pg2; 3 Q d3
       Kf1; 2 Ra8, any; 3 Ra1

No. 7
1 Ba4 *waiting*
       Bb6; 2 Sd6, any; 3 S × Pc4
       Bb8; 2 Sd4, P × S; 3 BP × P
                   else; 3 Sc6
       Rh1; 2 Sg6 ck, Kd5; 3 Sc7
       Bf7, h7; 2 Sd6
       Sb6; 2 S × B, any; 3 Sc6
       Sb8; 2 Sd6, any; 3 S × Pc4

85

No. 8

1 Kd2 *threat* 2 Bg4 ck, S × B; 3 Rh5
    Q checks; 2 K × Q or S × Q
    Q e8; 2 B × Q

No. 9

1 Q a5 *waiting*

No. 10

1 Pb4 *threats* 2 Rd5 or Rf5
    Rc5 ck; 2 P × R, Pa2; 3 Pc6, Bc7; 4 P × P, any;
                                                5 P × S(Q)
    R × P; 2 S × R, Pa2; 3 Rd5, Pa1(Q); 4 S × Q, any; 5 Rd1

No. 11

1 B × P *threat* 2 B × P *threat* 3 Q c8 ck
                    Q × B ck; 3 K × Q
    P × B dis ck; 2 Pb7 *threat* 3 Q c8 ck
                    Q e6; 3 Q c8
    Q c5; 2 Q e8, Q c6; 3 Q × Q, P × Q; 4 Bc8
    Q c2; 2 Be2, Q × B; 3 Q c8 ck

No. 12

1 Q f1, Bb2; 2 Q b1 *threat* 3 Q × P
                    Pg6; 3 Q × B
    Bc3, d4; 2 Q d3
    Be5, f6; 2 Q f5
    Pg3; 2 Sg6 ck, P × S; 3 Q h3

No. 13

1 Q f8, Ph3; 2 S × P, Ka2; 3 S × P ck
    Kc4; 2 S × P, K × P; 3 S × P
                    K × S; 2 Q c5 ck
    K × B; 2 Sb4–c2 ck, Ka2; 3 Qa3 ck
    Pc2; 2 Sb4 × Pc2, any; 3 Q b4

No. 14

1 Bf8 *threat* 2 Q a1
    B × R; 2 B × Q
    K × R; 2 Q a3

No. 15

1 Ra6 *threat* 2 Q f1
    R × B; 2 R × R
    K × B; 2 Rf6
    P × B; 2 Bg5

No. 16
1 Ke2, Pf1(Q) dbl ck; 2 Ke3 *threat* 3 B or R dis ck
    Pf1(S) dis ck; 2 Rf2 dis ck, K×S; 3 Bd3 or Pd3
    K×S; 2 Bd3 ck, Kd4; 3 Rf4
    Kd4; 2 Rf4 ck, Pe5; 3 S×B
    Sc1 ck; 2 Ke3, Pf1(S) ck; 3 B×S or R×S
    Rd8; 2 Ke3
    Re7; 2 Rf7 dis ck, K×S; 3 Bd3 or Pd3

No. 17
1 Pf5, B×Rg8; 2 Rf7, B×R; 3 S×B
            K×S; 3 Be3
            B×S; 3 Bg7
    B×Rb7 ck; 2 K×B, B×S; 3 Bg7

No. 18
1 Sd3 *threat* 2 Rf5–f6 dbl ck, Kd5; 3 Rd6 or Rd7
    P×S or B×S; 2 Rf7–d7; K×R; 3 Rf7
                      Se7; 3 Rd6
                      Bc4 any ck; 3 Rf4
    Pg3 any ck; 2 Rf2 ck, Kd5; 3 Rd7
    Rd8; 2 Rf5–f6 dbl ck, Kd5; 3 Be6

No. 19
1 Rg2 *threat* 2 Qf3 ck
    Pb5; 2 Ke7, R×P; 3 Qf3 ck, K×Q; 4 Bd5
                            K else; 4 Qd5
            Rd1, c2; 3 Q×R
            R else; 3 Qc2 ck
            Pb4; 3 Qc4 ck

No. 20
1 Rg6 *threat* 2 Q×P ck
    Q×R; 2 Kb4, Qg1; 3 Ba8 *waiting*
                       Be3; 4 Bc3
                       else; 4 Q mates
    Q×P; 2 R×Pd6 ck, Kc4; 3 Bd5 ck, Kd4; 4 Q×S or P
                      Qd5; 3 B×Q, any; 4 Q×P
    Qd7, e7; 2 R×Pd6 ck, Q×R; 3 Q×P ck, Q any;
                                      4 Q×Q
    Qe5, f6; 2 Kb4

No. 21

1 Pb4 *threat* 2 Q e6 ck, Kd4; 3 Q e4
      P × P ep; 2 Se3, Kd4; 3 Q d7 ck, Kc5; 4 Sa4
                                        K × Se3; 4 Q × Pa7
                                        K × Sc3; 4 Q g7
                                        Ke5; 4 Sg4
                          Kd6; 3 Sb5 or Sc4 ck
                          Kf6; 3 Q e6
                          else; 3 Q c5 ck
            Rh6; 2 Q e8 ck, Kd6; 3 Q e7 ck
            Rh4; 2 Q e6 ck, Kd4; 3 Sb5 ck, Kc4; 4 Sd5–c3, c7
            Kd4; 2 Sb5 ck, K any; 3 Q e6

No. 22

1 Rg1 *waiting*
        Kg6; 2 Rh5 *threat* 3 Sf4 ck, P × S; 4 Kh4
                        K × R; 3 Bf7, any; 4 Sf4
                        Sd3; 3 Sh4 ck, K × R; 4 Bf3
                                      P × S ck; 4 K × P
        Pg4; 2 Sh4 ck, Kg5; 3 Pf4 ck, P × Pep; 4 K any
        Rc6 any; 2 Q × Rd7 ck, Kg6; 3 R × P ck, Kh5; 4 Q g4, h3
                            B × Q; 3 Se7
        Rf7; 2 Rh5, Kg6; 3 Sf4 or Sh4 ck

No. 23

1 Be7 *threat* 2 Q d3 ck, Ke5; 3 Q e4
        Ke5; 2 Bc6 *threat* 3 Bd6 ck, Kf5, f6; 4 Q f3
                                Kd4; 4 Q d3
                    P × B; 3 Bd6 ck, Kf5, f6; 4 Q f3
                                K else; 4 Q d3
                    Sc5; 3 Q × S ck, Kf4; 4 Q g5
                    Sf1 any; 3 Q e3 (×) ck, Kf5; 4 Q g5
                    Kf4; 3 Q f3 ck
                    else; 3 Bd6 ck

No. 24

1 Bh2 *threat* 2 Sf6
        Pc4; 2 Bd6, B × Pf3; 3 Sf5, B × R; 4 Sc7
                                K × R; 4 Sf6
                                else; 4 Sf6
                  Bd3; 3 Sf5
                  Se7; 3 Sf7
        Bc4 ck; 2 Ka1, B × P; 3 Sf6 ck, Kc6; 4 Re6
                        Se5; 3 R × S ck, Kd4; 4 Sf5
                        Sf4; 3 Sf6 ck, Kd6; 4 B × S

Se5; 2 R × S ck, Kc4; 3 Sd6 ck, Kd4; 4 Sh6–f5
                             Kd4; 3 Re4 or Sf5 ck
Sf4; 2 Sf6 ck, Kd6; 3 B × S

No. 25
1 Ba8 *threat* 2 Q × Pb4
    Bb8; 2 Bg1, Kc5; 3 Qd4 ck, K × Q; 4 Pf4
                Kc7; 3 Sf7, R any; 4 Qc4
                        else; 4 Q × R
                K × S; 3 Bh2 ck, Kf5; 4 Be4
                else; 3 Sf7 ck
    R × B; 2 Q × Pb4 ck, Kd5; 3 Qd2 ck, Kc5; 4 Pb4
                                 Ke4; 4 Qd3
    Kc5; 2 Qc4 ck, Kd6; 3 Q × P

No. 26
1 Bd2 *threat* 2 Ke7 *threat* 3 R × Pg5
                   Bb4 ck; 3 B × B
    B × B; 2 Bd5 *threat* 3 R × Pg5 ck, Kd6; 4 Se4
                  P × R; 3 R × Pg5 ck, K any; 4 Se4
                  P × P; 3 R × Pg5 ck, K × R; 4 Sh3
                                    Kd6; 4 Se4
                Bd3; 3 S × B ck, K × B; 4 R × Pd4
    Sb5; 2 Kd7, P × P; 3 R × Pg5 ck, K × R; 4 Sh3
                P × R; 3 P × Pf4 ck, Kf5; 4 Be4
    P × P; 2 B × B ck, K × R; 3 Rf6 ck, Kg3; 4 Be5
    Be6; 2 Sd3 ck, Kd6; 3 Rf4–f6, any; 4 R × B
    Bf1; 2 R × Pg5 ck, Ke6; 3 Bd5 ck, Kd6; 4 Se4
    P × R; 2 P × Pf4 ck, Kf5; 3 Be4
    Pc1(Q); 2 Ke7, Qg1; 3 Re6 ck, B × R; 4 Sd3
                  Bb4 ck; 3 B × B, Q × P; 4 Bd6

No. 27
1 Sa4 *threat* 2 Sd4 ck, Kd5; 3 Rc5 ck, Ke4; 4 Sc3
    Kd5; 2 Rb1, K × P; 3 Sb6, K × S; 4 Sd4
                                Kb7; 4 S × Pa5
                Ke4; 3 Sc3 ck, Kf3; 4 Rf1
                Kc4; 3 Sb6 ck, Kb5; 4 Sd4
                Ke6; 3 Sb6, any; 4 Sd4
                Se4; 3 Sb6 ck, K × P; 4 S × Pa5
                                  Ke6; 4 Sd4
                else; 3 Sc3 ck
    P × P; 2 Sb3–c5 ck, Kd5; 3 Sb6
    Se4; 2 Sd4 ck, Kd5; 3 Sb6

No. 28

1 Bg4 *threat* 2 S × Pb3 ck, K × R; 3 Q × Pf4 ck, K × S; 4 Pc4
threat 2 Rc4 ck, K × Re5; 3 Q × Pf4 ck, K × S;
      4 Q × Pe4 ck, Kd6; 5 Rc6
  P × Q; 2 Rd6, P × R; 3 Sc3, K × R; 4 Sc6 ck
        P × R; 4 Sb5 ck
        Q × R; 4 Se2 ck
        P × P; 4 Rd5 ck
        Pd5; 4 R × Pd5 ck
        Re8; 4 Rd5 ck
        Ke3; 4 Sc4 ck
    K × R; 3 Sc4 ck, Kd4; 4 S × Pc7 ck
    Q × R; 3 Sc6 ck, Kc4; 4 Se3 ck
    B × S; 3 Sb6 dis ck, P × R; 4 Rd5 ck
    Ra8; 3 Sb6 dis ck, P × R; 4 Rd5 ck
    R × B; 3 Sc6 ck, Kc4; 4 Se3 ck
    P × P; 3 S × Pc7 ck
  R × B; 2 S × Pe3, P × S; 3 Rd6 ck, P × R; 4 Sc6
          K × R; 4 Sc4
      K × R; 3 Sa5–c4 ck, Kd4; 4 Qd2
      Rd8; 3 S × R dis ck
  S × B; 2 Rd6, K × R; 3 Sc4 ck, Kd4; 4 S × Pc7
      Q × R; 3 Sc6 ck, Kc4; 4 Qe2
      B × S; 3 R × P ck, K × R; 4 Q × Pf4
      S × Q; 3 Se7 dis ck, K × R; 4 Sc4
          P × R; 4 Sc6
     P × P; 3 Se7 dis ck
  Sf3; 2 R × Pe4 ck or Rd6
  B × B; 2 Q × Pf4, Q × R; 3 Q × Pe3 ck, K × S; 4 Pc4
  Se6; 2 Rc6 × S, Q × R; 3 Qe2, Q × R; 4 Qd1 ck, Ke5;
             5 Sc4
        B × S; 4 Qd1 ck
     P × R; 3 Sc6 ck, Kc4; 4 Qe2
     B × S; 3 R × Pe4 ck
  Q × R; 2 Pc3 ck or Qe1
  K × R; 2 Q × Pf4 ck, Kd4; 3 Rc4 ck, K × S;
        4 Q × Pe4 ck, Kd6; 5 Rc6
       K × S; 3 Pc4 ck, Kd4;
       4 Rd6 ck, P × R; 5 Q × Pd6
  Pf5; 2 Q × Pf4, B × S; 3 Q × Pe3 ck, K × R;
        4 Qc3 ck, K × S; 5 Qc5
  Qh6; 2 Sf6, K × R; 3 Sc4 ck, Kd4; 4 Pc3 ck, Kd3; 5 Qe2
  B × S; 2 Pc3 ck, K × R; 3 Q × Pf4 ck, K × S; 4 Rc5

Re8; 2 S × B, K × R; 3 Sa5–c4 ck, Kd4; 4 Pc3 ck, Kd3;
5 Qe2
Ra8; 2 Rc4 ck, K × Re5; 3 Q × Pf4 ck, K × S;
4 Q × Pe4 ck, Kd6; 5 Rc6

No. 29
1 Pe8(R), K × P; 2 Pa8(S), Kb5; 3 Re5
Kc5; 2 Pa8(Q), Kb5; 3 Qd5
Kd6; 3 Qc6

No. 30
1 Pf6 × P, K × P; 2 Pe8(R), Kc6; 3 Re6
Kf6; 2 Pe8(B), Ke6; 3 Rh6
Kd7; 2 Pe8(Q) ck, K × P; 3 Qd7 or g6

No. 31
1 Be2, Kb7; 2 Qc8 ck, K × Q; 3 Ba6
Ka7; 3 Qb8
Kb6; 3 Qc7
Kb6; 2 Qa5 ck, K × Q; 3 Bc7
Kb7; 3 Qa6
Kc6; 3 Bf3
Pb3; 2 Qd7 ck, Kb6; 3 Qc7
Kc5; 3 Qd6

No. 32
1 Ra5, Kg4; 2 Qb3, K × P; 3 Qg8, Kh3; 4 R × P
Kf4; 3 Qd3, Kg4; 4 Ra4

No. 33
1 Rg1, Kh6; 2 Kf5, Kh5; 3 Rh1
Ph6; 2 Rg2, Kh4; 3 Rh2

No. 34
1 Rc2, Pg1(Q); 2 Q × Q ck
else; 2 R × P

No. 35
1 Bb6, Pe3; 2 S × P ck, Kd6; 3 Sf5 ck, Kd5; 4 Ba5, Kc5, 5 Re5;
Kd6; 2 R × P, Kd5; 3 Sf6 ck, Kd6; 4 Ba6, Kc6; 5 Re6

No. 36
1 Rb7, Sd4 ck; 2 Kb6, Se6; 3 Rh7, any; 4 Rh8
Se5 ck; 2 Kc7, Sc4; 3 Rb1, any; 4 Ra1

No. 37

1 Bh3, K any; 2 Qg4, any; 3 Qc8
       Pa5; 2 Qa6 ck, K×Q; 3 Bc8
               else; 3 Qc8

No. 38

1 Sb3 *waiting*
     Sa2; 2 Qb2 ck, S×Q; 3 Sa3
     Kc2; 2 Sd4 ck, Kb1; 3 Sd2
               Kd1; 3 Qa1
     Sd3; 2 Qa1 ck, Kc2; 3 Sd4
     Sd5; 2 Sd4 *threat* 3 Sd2
              Sb2; 3 Q×S
     Sc6; 2 Se3, any; 3 Qa1

No. 39

1 Ke2, Ra1; 2 Be4 ck, Ka2; 3 Qg8
     Ra2 ck; 2 Bd2 dis ck, K any; 3 Qc1
     Re6 ck; 2 Be3 dis ck, K any; 3 Qc1
     Rf6; 2 Bf4 dis ck, K any; 3 Qc1
     Rg6; 2 Bg5 dis ck, K any; 3 Qc1
     Kc2; 2 Qd1 ck, Kb1; 3 Ba3
               Kc3; 3 Qb3
     else; 2 Bd2 dis ck

No. 40

1 Ka8, Pa2; 2 Ba7 *threat* 3 Qh3
            Kg3; 3 Qf2
     Pe4; 2 Ba6, any; 3 Qf1
     Kg3; 2 Ba7 *threat* 3 Qf2
            Kg3; 3 Qh3

No. 41

1 Bf5, Kf1; 2 Bg4, Kf2; 3 Bd2, Kg3; 4 Be1
                         Kf1; 4 Rf4
     Kf3; 2 Kg1, Ke2; 3 Bc2, Kf3; 4 Bd1
                         Ke1; 4 Re4
     Ke2; 2 Kg2, Ke1; 3 Bd3, Kd1; 4 Ra1
     Ke1; 2 Kg2, Ke2; 3 Bc2, Ke1; 4 Re4

No. 42

1 Rf5, Ba3; 2 Rf1 ck, Ka2; 3 Q×P
               Bc1; 3 Qb2
     Ka2; 2 Ra5 ck, Kb1; 3 Qf5
               Ba3; 3 Qb2
     Kc2; 2 Rb5

No. 43
1 Ra2, Qc7, h2; 2 Ra8 ck, Qb8; 3 R×Q
   Qc8, g8; 2 Rh2 ck, Qh3; 3 R×Q

No. 44
1 Bb1, Ka3,b3; 2 Sc2(ck), K any; 3 Rb4
   K×B; 2 Bc3, any; 3 Rf1
   Pg3; 2 Bc2, Ka1; 3 Bc3
        Ka3; 3 Bc1

No. 45
1 Qd1, Pg1(S); 2 Sf2 ck, Kh2; 3 Qd6
   Pg1(Q); 2 Qf3 ck, Kh2; 3 Qh5
   Kh2; 2 Sf3 ck, Kh3; 3 Qd7

No. 46
1 Sc4, Pb1(Q); 2 Qa8 ck, Qa2; 3 Rc1
   Pb1(S); 2 Qb8
   Pf1(Q); 2 Qa8 ck, Kb1; 3 Sd2
   Pf1(S); 2 Qe1 ck, Pb1(Q); 3 Ra3

No. 47
1 Sc7, Kb8; 2 Sa6 ck, Ka7; 3 Pb8(S)
   K×P; 2 Kb5, K any; 3 Sa6

No. 48
1 Kh4, Kd4; 2 Qd2 ck, Kc4; 3 Sc5, K×S; 4 Qc3
        Ke5; 3 Qd6 ck, Kf5; 3 Se7
   Kf6; 2 Qg5 ck, Ke6; 3 Sd6, K×S; 4 Qf6
        Kf7; 3 Bd5 ck, Ke8; 4 Qe7

No. 49
1 Sh3, Kf3; 2 Be2 ck, Ke3; 3 Qd3
        Ke4; 3 Qe6
   Kg4; 2 Kg2, Kf5; 3 Qe6
        Kh5; 3 Be2
   Pd3; 2 Be6, Kf3; 3 Qd3
   K×S; 2 Qg6

No. 50
1 Rg4–g7, Kd4; 2 Rg7–e7, Kd5; 3 Sf4 ck, Kd4; 4 Rb4
              Kc4; 4 Re4
              Kd6; 4 Re6
              Kc6; 4 Rb6
        Kd3; 3 Sf4 ck, Kc2; 4 Re7–c7
   Kd6; 2 Rg7–e7, Kc6; 3 Sf4, Kd6; 4 Re6
   Ke4, e6; 2 Rb7–d7, Ke5; 3 Sc5, Kf5; 4 Rd5
            Kf5; 3 Sc5, Ke5; 4 Rg5
   Ke5; 2 Rb7–d7, K any; 3 Sc5

No. 51

1 Pf6, K×S; 2 P×P, Kf6; 3 Pg8(R), Ke6; 4 Rg8–g6
Pg6; 2 Pf7, K×S; 3 Pf8(R), Kd6; 4 Rf6
P×P; 2 Rb6 ck, Kd7; 3 Rg7 ck, Kc8; 4 Rc7
Ke8; 4 Rb8

No. 52

1 Qb1, P×B; 2 Qg1, Kh3; 3 S×P, Ph4; 4 Sg5
Pf2; 3 Qg2, Pf1; 4 Sg6
Kg3; 2 Qg1 ck, Kh3; 3 Bg4 ck, Kh4; 4 S×Pf3
Kf4; 3 Sd3 ck, Ke4; 4 B×Pg6
Kf5; 4 Q×P
K×B; 2 Qg1
else; 2 Q×P

No. 53

1 Ra4, B×R; 2 Pb4 ck, P×P ep; 3 Kb2, Bb5; 4 Sd6–b7
Bc6; 4 S×P
Sc6; 4 Sa5–b7
Bb3, e2; 2 R×P ck, B×R; 3 Pb4

No. 54

1 Kh5, Ba2; 2 Kh6, Bb3; 3 Kh7, Ba4; 4 Kh8, B×B; 5 Qh7

No. 55

1 Qf1 *threat* 2 Ke2
Sc4; 2 Qd3 ck, K×Q; 3 Bb1
Sd5; 2 Qf3 ck, K×Q; 3 B×S
Se6; 2 Qf5 ck, K×Q; 3 Bb1
Sd8 else; 2 Bb1 ck, Kd5; 3 Qf7(×)
Bf4; 2 Q×B ck, Kd3; 3 Qf5
Be3; 2 Qe2 *threat* 3 Qc2
Kf5; 3 Qg4
Bd2 ck; 2 K×B

No. 56

1 Pa8(Q), B×S; 2 Q×S ck, K×Q; 3 Qd3
S×Pb4; 2 Qe4 ck, K×Q; 3 Qc4
S×Pf4; 2 Qc4 ck, K×Q; 3 Qe4
R×B; 2 Qd3 ck, K×Q; 3 Q×S

No. 57

1 Be5, Bh1; 2 B×P, any; 3 Bd6, any; 4 Bf8, any; 5 Bg7

No. 58

1 Q b7 *threat* 2 Q c6 *threat* 3 Q c5 ck
    Sf5; 2 Q d5 ck, S × Q; 3 Re4 ck, K × R; 4 Re6
    Se6; 2 Q e4 ck, S × Q; 3 Rf5 ck, K × R; 4 Rd5
    Sg7 × P; 2 Q c6, Sg3 ck; 3 Kg2, Re8; 4 Q × P

No. 59

1 Rb4 *threat* 2 Pd4 ck, P × P ep; 3 Re4 or Q a1
                   K × P; 3 Q a1 or Q f6
    P × R; 2 Pd4 ck, P × P ep; 3 Q a1
            K × P; 3 Q f6
    Bb1; 2 Pd4 ck, P × P ep; 3 Re4

No. 60

1 Pd7 *threat* 2 Rf8 *threat* 3 Q d6 or Pd8(S)
              R × S; 3 P × R(Q)
    R × S; 2 Q d5 ck, K × Q; 3 P × R(Q)
             Ke7; 3 P × R(S)

No. 61

1 Kf5, S × R ck; 2 Kg5, S any; 3 Sc7
    S × B; 2 Bf3, S any; 3 B × P
            P × R; 3 Re5
    Sb2; 2 Bf3
    Sc3; 2 R × S, Pe3; 3 Bf3

No. 62

1 Se3, K × P; 2 Bd3 ck, Ka4; 3 Sc4, Kb5; 4 Sb2
    Ka3; 2 Bd3, Ka4; 3 Sc4, K × P; 4 Sb2
           Ka2; 3 Sc2, Kb1; 4 Sb4

No. 63

1 Qf2 *threat* 2 Q a7 ck
    B × Q; 2 Sf4–e6 *threat* 3 Sf8
              Bc5; 3 S × B
    R × Q; 2 Sd5 *threat* 3 Sb6
           Rf6; 3 S × R

No. 64

1 Qf7 *threat* 2 Q a2
    Bd5; 2 Q a7, Ra4; 3 Q h7, Be4; 4 Q h4
                          Re4; 4 Q h1

No. 65

1 Be4 *threat* 2 Qd5
　　K×B; 2 Re3
　　R×B; 2 R×P
　　B×B; 2 Pf4
　　Rd4; 2 Qe7

No. 66

1 Qa6 *threat* 2 Rd1
　　Pe1(Q); 2 Rf3
　　Rb7 ck; 2 Bb6
　　Pd5 dis ck; 2 Be5
　　Re4 ck; 2 Bd4
　　Ke1; 2 Qa1

No. 67

1 Rc1–c7 *threat* 2 Sc3
　　Sc2; 2 Pb4
　　S×P; 2 R×B
　　Sb5; 2 Rc5
　　Sc6; 2 Rc7–d7
　　Se6; 2 Re7–d7
　　Sf5; 2 Re5
　　Sf3; 2 Qe4
　　Se2; 2 Q×R

No. 68

1 Sd4 *threat* 2 Rg4
　　K×S; 2 Qb4
　　Q×S; 2 Q×Ph7
　　B×S; 2 Qb1
　　P×S; Q×Pd5

No. 69

1 Bh7 *threat* 2 Qd8 ck, Ke5; 3 Sd3
　　Ke5; 2 Qc7 ck, Kf6; 3 Sg4
　　　　　　　　　K else; 3 Qc5
　　Kd4; 2 Qd2 ck, Ke5; 3 Sg4
　　Pe5; 2 Bg8 ck, Kd4; 3 Qd2
　　　　　　　　　Kd6; 3 Qd8

No. 70

1 Rc2 *threat* 2 Sc6 ck
　　Sd3; 2 Qe3 ck, K×Q; 3 Sf5
　　　　　　　　　S×Q; 3 Sc6
　　Kc5; 2 Qa3 ck, Kb5; 3 Bc6
　　　　　　　　　Kd4; 3 Sf5
　　Pb5; 2 Sf5 ck, Kc5; 3 Qd6
　　Se3; 2 Qf4 ck, Kd3; 3 Qe4

No. 71

1 Bd7, Se3; 2 Se8, K×R; 3 Sf6
　　Sb2; 2 R×Pb4, B×R; 3 Pe4
　　Sc3, f2; 2 Rf4 *threat* 3 Rf5
　　　　　　　　　K×S; 3 Rd4
　　Pb5; 2 Rc4 *threat* 3 Rc5 or Pe4
　　Pf5; 2 Be6 ck, Kc6; 3 Rc4
　　Rd3; 2 P×R, any; 3 Rd4

No. 72

1 Bb8 *threat* 2 Se5 *threats* 3 Qc4, c6, d6
                    Kc5; 3 Qa5
     Pe3; 2 Qc8, any; 3 Sf6
     Rd1; 2 Ba7, Pe3; 3 Sc3
     Rc3; 2 Sf6 ck, Kc5; 3 Bd6
     Kc5; 2 Qa5 ck, K any; 3 Se5

No. 73

1 Rg3, Sc8; 2 Qe3 ck (*threat*), P×Q; 3 Rg4 ck, Kf5; 4 Sh6
     Pe5; 2 Qc3 (*threat*), B×Q; 3 Sd6 ck, Kd4; 4 Bd3
     Bc6; 2 Qd2, B×Q; 3 Sd6 ck, Kd4, d5; 4 Rd3
                     P×R; 3 Sf6 ck, Kf5; 4 Qg5
     Bc4; 2 Sf6 ck, Kf5; 3 Q ×Pf4 ck, K×Q; 4 Rf3
               Kd4; 3 Q ×Pf4 ck, Kc5; 4 Qd6
     Kf5; 2 Sh6 ck, Ke4; 3 Qe3 ck, P×Q; 4 Rg4
     P×R; 2 Sf6 ck, Kd4; 3 Pe3 ck, Kd3; 4 Se5

No. 74

1 Bc4 *threat* 2 Qf6 ck, S×Q; 3 Sf7 ck, Kf5; 4 Se7
     Kd6; 2 Qe7 ck, S×Q; 3 Sf7 ck, Kd7; 4 Sf6
     Rg6; 2 Qf4 ck, S×Q; 3 Sf7 ck, Kf5; 4 Pe4
     Rh8; 2 Qe6 ck, S×Q; 3 Sf7 ck, Kf5; Bd3

No. 75

1 Pe7 *threats* 2 Be6 ck, Pe8(Q) or Rf4
     Pf5; 2 Q×B ck, K×Q; 3 R ×Pf5 ck, Ke4; 4 Pf3
                              Kd6; 4 Bc5
     Ke4; 2 Qd8, B×Q; 3 Re3 ck, Kf4; 4 P×P
                       Kd5; 4 Be6
     S×P, Rg6, Rh7; 2 Rf4, B×Q; 3 Rd4 ck, Ke5; 4 Pf4
     B×Q; 2 Rd3 ck, Ke5; 3 B×B ck, Ke4; 4 Pf3
              Ke4; 3 Pf3 ck, Ke4; 4 B×B
              Kc4; 3 Rd4 ck
     Kc4; 2 Rf4 ck or Be6 ck

No. 76

1 Q e2, Q × Q ; 2 Sg7, B × S; 3 P × S ck, K × Pe6; 4 Sc7 ck, Ke5;
5 P × Pf4

B × P; 3 Sf5 ck, K × P; 4 Sc7
S × S; 4 Rd8–e8

S × S ck; 2 Q × S, Q × Q; 3 P × B ck, K × Pe6; 4 Sg7 ck,
Ke5; 5 P × Pd4

R × S; 2 Qg4, B × P; 3 Rd8–e8 ck, S × R; 4 Rf7 ck, K d8;
5 Pe7

R × P; 3 Rf8–e8 ck, S × R; 4 Rd7ck, Kf8;
5 Rf7

S × S ck; 3 Kb7, B × P; 4 Rf7 ck, K × Rd8;
5 Qg8

Sc6 ck; 4 P × S, Sd6 ck;
5 P × S

R × P; 2 S × S, K × P; 3 S × Pf4 ck, K × P; 4 Sc4 ck, Kf5;
5 Rd5

No. 77

1 Rc1 *threat* 2 Kd1
P × R(Q) ck; 2 K × Q
Pd1(Q) ck; 2 K × Q
P × P ck; 2 Kd1
Sb2; 2 K × S
Sc3; 2 K × S
Pe2; 2 K × P
Q × R; 2 R × Q
Pe5; 2 Qd7

No. 78

1 Pg4 *waiting*
R × S; 2 Q × R
(added mate)

No. 80

1 Rb4, Q × Q; 2 Be4
Qd5; 2 Bb5
Qd4; 2 Rb3
Pe5; 2 Qh3
B any; 2 Qh7

No. 82

1 Bc5, S × Q dis ck; 2 Bd3
Sb5 dis ck; 2 Bd3
Sf5 dis ck; 2 Bd5
S × P, S × B, Sf7 dis ck;
2 Sd4

No. 79

1 Kc3 *waiting*
Bg3; 2 Sc5
B × S; 2 R × B
B else; 2 Qf4(×)
Rg3; 2 Qf4
Rf3; 2 P × R
Re3; 2 Qf5
Rh3 × S ck; 2 P × R
Rh4; 2 Sc5
Rd6 × S ck; 2 P × R
Rd4; 2 Q × R
Rd5; 2 B × R
B × P; 2 B × B

No. 81

Bb2 *threat* 2 Bd4
Sa4; 2 P × S
Sa6; 2 Pb4
Sb7; 2 P × P
Sd7; 2 P × S
S × Pe6; 2 Q × Q
Se4; 2 Sf1
Sd3; 2 Re2
S × Pb3; 2 Q × S

No. 83
1 Qa1, Q × Q ck; 2 Pc3
    Qb2 ck; 2 Bc3
    Q × B; 2 Q × B
    Bb2 ck; 2 Pc3

No. 85
1 Qh5, P × Q; 2 Sf5
    K × S; 2 Bc5
    Sa1 any; 2 Sc2(×)
    Se5; 2 Bc5
    Sd3 else; 2 Qh8

No. 86
1 Qd2 *threat* 2 Qh2
    Kd6; 2 Sc4
    Q × Q; 2 Sc4
    Q × B; 2 Qd4
    Qe3; 2 Qd6
    Pg4; 2 Qf4

No. 87
1 Sf5, Pg5; 2 Bg4, K × P; 3 Sc5
        Pc3; 3 Se3
   K × P; 2 Sc5 ck, K × S; 3 Qh3
   P × S; 2 Qd1 ck, K × P; 3 Qd6
   Pc3; 2 Qb1, K × P; 3 Sc5
       Kc4; 3 Se3
       else; 3 Qa2
   Pa6; 2 Qh3, P × P; 3 Se7
       Pc3; 3 Se3
       K × P; 3 Sc5
       P × S; 3 Q × P
   Sf7; 2 K × S, P × S; 3 Qd1
       Pc3; 3 Se3

No. 84
1 Qc3 *threat* 2 Se2
    Rd4; 2 Qe3
    Bf3; 2 Sd3
    Qe3; 2 Q × Q
    Qd4, f2; 2 S × P

No. 88
1 Sa3 *threat* 2 Sc2
    K × R dis ck; 2 Se4
    R × P dis ck; 2 Sc3–b5
    Rd6, e7 dis ck; 2 Pc6
    Rh2; 2 Re4

No. 89
1 Se3 *threat* 2 Qf1
    S × P dis ck; 2 Sg4
    S else dis ck; 2 Pd4

No. 90
1 Be4 *threat* 2 Q × P
    K × B; 2 Rc4
    P × B; 2 Qd8
    Re2 × B; 2 Rc1

    Q × B; 2 Rc2
    Rf4 × B; 2 Sf5
    Sf2 × B; 2 Rh3–d3
    Sg5 × B; 2 Se6

No. 91

1 Bh6 *threat* 2 Se6
    Q×P; 2 Sc2
    R×P; 2 Qa7
    S×Pe4; 2 Qf2
    S×Pf3 ck; 2 S×S

No. 92

1 Sa5 *threat* 2 Rc4
    Sb4; 2 S×P
    Sb6; 2 S×P
    S×B; 2 Q×S
    Se7; 2 Bd6
    Sf6; 2 Q×Bf8
    Sf4; 2 Q×Q
    Se3; 2 Qd4
    Sc3; 2 S×Pd3

No. 93

1 R×B ck, Ke3; 2 Bd5, Q×B; 3 Sf5 ck, Q×S; 4 Sc4
               Rb5×B; 3 Sd1 ck, R×S; 4 Sf5
               Rd7×B; 3 Sf5 ck, R×S; 4 Sd1

Nc. 94

1 Qf3, S×P; 2 Rg7, Rg8×R; 3 Bc7 ck, R×B; 4 Qg3
            Rh7×R; 3 Qg3 ck, R×Q; 4 Bc7

No. 95

1 Bh6, Rf2; 2 Sf3, Rh3×S; 3 Bf8 ck, R×B; 4 R×P
          Rf2×S; 3 R×P ck, R×R; 4 Bf8
    Rd2; 2 Sd3, Rh3×S; 3 Bf8 ck, Rd6; 4 R×P
          Rd2×S; 3 R×P ck, R×R; 4 Bf8

No. 96

1 Ra2, Rf2; 2 Be2, Rf2×B; 3 Re8 ck, R×Re8; 4 Rc2
            Rel×B; 3 Rc2 ck, R×Rc2; 4 Re8
    Qf1; 2 Be2, Q×B; 3 Re8 ck, Q×Re8; 4 Rc2
          R×B; 3 Rc2 ck, R×Rc2; 4 Re8
    Rf4; 2 Se4, Rf4×Se4; 3 Re8 ck, R×R; 3 Rc2
          Rel×S; 3 Rc2 ck, Rc4; 4 Re8
    Qh7; 2 Se4
    Rf5; 2 Se5
    Pd5; 2 Se6

No. 97

1 Se5 *threat* 2 Qb2
    Rc4–d4; 2 Qd5, R×Q; 3 S×P
    Rd3–d4; 2 Qe4, R×Q; 3 Sd7

No. 98

1 Be7 *threat* 2 Ba3
    Rb5–c5; 2 Sc4 ck, R×S; 3 Bg5
    Rc6–c5; 2 Bg5 ck, R×B; 3 Sc4

No. 99

1 Bb3 *threat* 2 S × R ck
    Rf8–f6; 2 Sc6 ck, R × S; 3 Q f4
    Rg6–f6; 2 Sf3 ck, R × S; 3 Q e6
    Q d6; 2 Sc6 ck, Q × S; 3 Q d4
    Rd6; 2 Q d4 ck, R × Q; 3 Sc6

No. 100

1 Bh4 *threat* 2 B × R ck
    Re6; 2 Pe3 ck, R × P; 3 Sc6
    Q e6; 2 Sc6 ck, Q × S; 3 Pe3
    Rf6–d6; 2 R × Pd5 ck, R × R; 3 Sc6
    Rd7–d6; 2 Sc6 ck, R × S; 3 R × Pd5

No. 101

1 Ba8 *threat* 2 Pd4 dis ck
    Bf7; 2 Pe6, Q × Pe6; 3 Pd4 dis ck, Q × R; 4 R × P
             B × P; 3 R × P ck, B × R; 4 Pd4
    Bg6; 2 Pf5, Q × Pf5; 3 Pd4 dis ck, Q d3; 4 R × P
             B × P; 3 R × P ck, B × R; 4 Pd4

No. 102

1 Q d2 *threat* 2 Q d8 ck
    Bd4; 2 Pc5 ck, B × P; 3 Q d8
    Q d4; 2 Q h6 ck, Q f6; 2 Pc5

No. 103

1 Ra3–a1 *threat* 2 Ra1–d1 ck
    Q h5; 2 Bg4, B × B; 3 Ra1–d1 ck, B × R; 4 Q d7
              Q × B; 3 Q d7 ck, Q × Q; 4 Ra1–d1
    Q × S or Q g6; 2 Bf5, B × B; 3 Ra1–d1 ck, Bd3; 4 Q d7
                      Q × B; 3 Q d7 ck, Q × Q;
                                4 Ra1–d1
    Q g7; 2 Sf6, B × S; 3 Ra1–d1 ck, Bd4; 4 Q e7
              Q × S; 3 Q e7 ck, Q × Q; 4 Ra1–d1
    Pf3; 2 Sg5, B × S; 3 Ra1–d1 ck, Bd2; 4 Q e7
              Q × S; Q e7 ck, Q × Q; 4 Ra1–d1
    R × R; 2 S × P ck, Kd5; 3 Re5 ck, K × S; 4 Q × Pc5

No. 104

1 Sd8 *threat* 2 P × R dis ck
    Rc4–c5; 2 S × P ck, R × S; 3 Sc6
    Rd5–c5; 2 Sc6 ck, R × S; 3 S × P
    Q g4; 2 Se2 ck, Q × S; 3 Se6
    Bg4; 2 Se6 ck, B × S; 3 Se2

No. 105

1 Bc3 *threat* 2 Re5
     Rb5; 2 Qb7 ck, R×Q; 3 Re5
     Qb5; 2 Qa4 ck, Q×Q; 3 Re5
     Bd5; 2 Qe6 ck, B×Q; 3 Re5
     Qd5; 2 Qc4 ck, Q×Q; 3 Re5

No. 106

1 Bg2 *threat* 2 Q×Pe5 ck, P×Q; 3 B×Pe5
     Qb5; 2 Se2 ck, Q×S; 3 Sc6
     Bb5; 2 Sc6 ck, B×S; 3 Se2
     Rf8–f6; 2 Se6 ck, R×S; 3 S×P
     Rg6–f6; 2 S×P ck, R×S; 3 Se6

No. 107

1 Pc5 *threat* 2 Pc6, B×P; 3 Se6
               R×P; 3 Q×Pf3
     Ra6–d6; 2 Q×Pd2 ck, R×Q; 3 Se6
     Rd8–d6; 2 Se6 ck, R×S; 3 Q×Pd2
     Be4; 2 R×Pf5 ck, B×R; 3 Q×Pf3
     Qe4; 2 Q×Pf3 ck, Q×Q; 3 R×Pf5
     Qd3; 2 Q×Pd2 ck, Q×Q; 3 R×Pf5

No. 108

1 Sg5 *waiting*
     Rg8–g7; 2 Sf7 ck, R×S; 3 S×Pg6
     Rh7–g7; 2 S×Pg6 ck, R×S; 3 Sf7
     Be2; 2 S×Pd3 ck, B×S; 3 S×Pf3
     Qe2; 2 S×Pf3 ck, Q×S; 3 S×Pd3

No. 109

1 Rb5, K×P; 2 Ke3, K×R; 3 Rc5, Ke1; 4 Rc1
        Kc4; 2 Rd1–d5, Kc3; 3 Rd5–c5 ck, Kd4; 4 Pc3
                 Pe3; 3 K×P, any; 4 Rd5–c5
     Pe3; 2 Rd1–d5, Pe4; 3 Rd5–c5 ck, Kd4; 4 Pc3

No. 110

1 Pg8(R), Ka3; 2 Rb4, Ka2; 3 Ra8
        Kb1; 2 Rg2, Ka1; 3 Rc1
        Kb3; 2 Rg2, Ka3; 3 Rc3

No. 111

1 Rh7, Sd4; 2 Ra7, Se6; 3 Ra7–b7 *threats* 4 Rb8 or Rh8
        Sd6; 2 Ra7, Kd8; 3 Rh7–g7 *threats* 4 Ra8 or Rg8

No. 112
1 Rd2, Sg1 ck; 2 Kg3, Sh3; 3 Re2, Sg1; 4 R×P
            else; 4 Re1
       Sf3; 3 K×S, Kg1; 4 Rd1
       Se2; 3 R×S, Kg1; 4 Re1
     Sc3; 2 Rc2, Sa2; 3 R×S, Kg1; 4 Ra1
       Se2; 3 R×S, Kg1; 4 Re1
       Sd1; 3 Rc1, Kg1; 4 R×S

No. 113
1 Rf6, Sh3; 2 R×P (*threat*), S any; 3 Rg8
          P×R; 3 R×S
          Ph5, h6; 3 Rh6(×)
    Ph5; 2 R×Ph5 ck, P×R; 3 Rh6

No. 114
1 Rg2, Rb1; 2 Rc2–d2, any; 3 Rg2–e2
    Rc1; 2 Rg2–e2 ck, Kd1; 3 Rc2–d2
    Kd1; 2 Kf1, any; 3 Rg2–d2

No. 115
1 Rh3, Pg4; 2 Rh2, Ke3; 3 Ke5, any; 4 Pd4
       Pg3; 3 Re2, Pg2; 4 Re4
    P×P; 2 Ke6, Kc5; 3 R×P, Kc6; 4 Rc4

No. 116
1 Ra3, Pc2; 2 Kf5, Pg3; 3 R×Pg3, any; 4 Rh3
         else; 3 Rh3 ck, P×R; 4 R×P
    P×P; 2 Rb3, Pc2; 3 R×Pd4, Pc1; 4 Rh3
       Pg3; 3 Re3, P×R; 4 R×Pb4,
           else; 4 Re4
    Pc4; 2 Ra3×P, P×(either)R; 3 R×Pc3 or d3, Pg3;
              4 Rc4 or d4
    Pg3; 2 Re3, P×R; 3 R×P, any; 4 Rc4

No. 117
1 Qb1 *threat* 2 Qb4
   Qd3; 2 P×Q
   Q×R; 2 Pc3
   Qe5, g5; 2 Pc4
   Qb3; 2 P×Q

No. 118
1 Se3, Kg5; 2 Pg3, Kh5; 3 Sg1, any; 4 Sf3, any; 5 Pg4
     Kh4; 2 Kg6, Pc4; 3 Sd1, any; 4 Sf2, any; 5 Pg3
    Pc4; 2 Pg3, any; 3 Sg1

No. 119

1 Pc6 *threat* 2 Re8 ck
         Q e7 ck; 2 Pg5 dis ck, Pf5; 3 P × P ep
         Q d6; 2 Re8 ck, Kd5; 3 Re5
         Q × P ck; 2 B × Q ck, Pf5; 3 Re8
         Q × B; 2 Re8 ck, Kf6; 3 R × Pf7

No. 120

1 Q a3 *threat* 2 Pe4 ck, P × P ep; 3 Q d3
                         K × P; 3 Sg5
         R × Q; 2 Pe4 ck, P × P ep; 3 Sg3
                         K × P; 3 Sg5
         B × P; 2 Q × R ck, Bg4; 3 Q d3
         Bf3; 2 Q d3 ck, Be4; 3 Q × R

No. 121

1 Ph4 *threat* 2 B × Pf4 ck, K × B; 3 Sd3
                        Kf6; 3 Sd5
         P × P ep; 2 Pg4 *threat* 3 Sf7
                   P × P ep; 3 Pf4

No. 122

1 Pd4 *threat* 2 Pd5 ck, P × P; 3 B × Pd5
         Pd5; 2 B × Pc6, any; 3 B × Pd5
         Pc4 × P ep; 2 Q a2 ck, Pd5; Pc5 × P ep
         Pe4 × P ep; 2 Pf4 *threat* 3 Pf5
                   Pf5; 3 P × P ep

No. 123

1 Q g2 *threat* 2 Q g7 ck
         Kd6; 2 Ba3 ck, Pc5; 3 P × P ep
                   Ke5; 3 Q g7
         Kf6; 2 Q g7 ck, K × Q; 3 Rg4
         Bg5; 2 Re4 dbl ck, Kd6; 3 Be5

No. 124

1 Pf3, B × S ck; 2 Pd4 ck (*threat*), P × P ep dis ck; 3 Kb4
         S × B; 2 Pd4 ck, P × P ep dis ck; 3 Q × R
         S × S; 2 Sg7, any; 3 B × R

No. 125

1 P × B(S), K × S; 2 Sb6, any; 3 Pa8(Q)

No. 126

1 Pf8(B), Kf6; 2 Rg3, Ke6; 3 Rg6

No. 127
1 Pd7, Kd6; 2 Pd8(S), P×B; 3 Rd7
      Kf7; 2 Pd8(Q) dis ck, Kg6; 3 Qg5
      P×P; 2 Pd8(R), Kf6; 3 Rd6
      P×B; 2 Pd8(B), Kd6; 3 Ra6

No. 128
1 Pa8(B), P×B(Q); 2 Pf8(Q), Q×P ck; 3 Pb5 ck, Q×P
                   Q×S; 3 Pb5 ck, Q×P
                   Q else; 3 White×Q
      P×B(R); 2 Pf8(R), R×S; 3 R×R, R×R
      P×B(B); 2 Pf8(B), B×P; 3 B×B, R×R
      P×B(S); 2 Pf8(S), S×Q; 3 R×S, R×R

No. 129
1 Bg4, Kc4; 2 Be6
      Se6; 2 Bf3
      Sd6; 2 Sb6
      Pc4; 2 Rh5

No. 130
1 Rg4, Ke6; 2 Rg5
      Se6; 2 Bf2
      Sd6; 2 Sc7
      Pc4; 2 Rg5

No. 131
1 Bc7 *waiting*
      Q any; 2 Qc6(×)
      Se8 any; 2 Qd6
      Sf8 any; 2 Qe8 or Be8
      Pb2; 2 Qa2
      Pe3; 2 Bf3

No. 132
1 Qal *threat* 2 Pc4
      Pb2; 2 Qa2
      Pe3; 2 Qhl

No. 133
1 Qa8, Pg3; 2 Qg2, any; 3 Q×Pg3
      Pe4; 2 Qa3, Pe3; 3 Q×P
               Pg3; 3 Q×P
               Ke5; 3 Qd6

No. 134
1 Qgl, Pf3; 2 Qf2, any; 3 Q×Pf3
      Pd4; 2 Qhl ck, Ke3; 3 Qel
               Pf3; 3 Q×P

No. 135
1 Rc8, Kf1; 2 Sf3 *threat* 3 Rcl ck
              Ph2; 3 S×Ph4, any; 4 Rcl
              Kg2; 3 Rg8 ck, any; 4 Rgl
      Kdl; 2 Sd3

No. 136

1 Re8 *threat* 2 Sc3 ck, Kc1; 3 Re2, any; 4 Rc2
    Kc1; 2 Re2, any; 3 Sc3 and 4 Rc2 or Ra2

No. 137

1 Sf5, Kc8; 2 Bd6, Kd8; 3 Bc7 ck, any; 4 Sd6
    Ke8; 2 Rb7, Kd8; 3 Be7 ck, any; 4 Sd6

No. 138

1 Sd3, Kc8; 2 Bb6, Kb8; 3 Sc5, any; 4 Rh8
    Ke8; 2 Bf6, Kf8; 3 Se5, any; 4 Rh8

No. 139

1 Be3, Kc8; 2 Bb6, Kb8; 3 Sc6 ck, Ka8; 4 Ra7
                                    Kc8; 4 Rc7
    Ke8; 2 Sc6, Kf8; 3 Bh6, Ke8; 4 Re7

No. 140

1 Sd3, Kc8; 2 Bb6, Kb8; 3 Sc5, any; 4 Rh8
    Ke8; 2 Bf6, Kf8; 3 Se5, any; 4 Rh8

No. 141 and 142

1 Ba4, K × S; 2 Bb3
        Pd6; 2 Sb5–c7
        Pf6; 2 Sd5–c7
        Pf5; 2 Qg8
        Pe4; 2 Q × Pe4

No. 143 and 144

1 Qc3, Sf2; 2 Qe5 ck, K × S; 3 Rg3
        Sg3; 2 Qe4 ck, K × S; 3 Rf2
        Kd5; 2 Rd2 ck, Ke4; 3 Rd4
                        Ke6; 3 Qe5
        Kf4; 2 Sd2, S any; 3 Qg3(×)
                Ph5; 3 Qd4
        Ph5; 2 Sg5 ck, Kd5; 3 Rd2
                Kf4; 3 Qd4

No. 145

1 Sd6, Qb6; 2 Rc1
        Qc6; 2 S × P
        Q × S; 2 Rc3
        Q else; 2 Rb5 or Sd6–b7

        S any; 2 Se4(×)
        Pe5; 2 Rd5

No. 146

1 Sd6, Qb6; 2 Qc2, c3, c4
        Qc6; 2 S × P
        Q × S; 2 Rc3
        Q else; 2 Qb5 or
                        Sd6–b7
        S any; 2 Se4(×)
        Pe5; 2 Rd5

No. 147
1 Kg7, Bg2; 2 Rf4, any; 3 Rf8
      Be2; 2 Rb4–b7, any; 3 Sb6
      Bg4; 2 Rd7–b7, any; 3 Sc7
      B × S; 2 R × B, Ka7; 3 Ra5
      Be4; 2 R × B, Kb8; 3 Re8

No. 148
1 Rb4, Bf3; 2 Rf4, any; 3 Rf8
      Bf1; 2 Rb4–b7, any; 3 Sb6
      Bh3; 2 Rd7–b7, any; 3 Sc7
      B × B; 2 R × B, Ka7; 3 Ra5
      Be4; 2 R × B, Kb8; 3 Re8
      Ph4; 2 Rf4, any; 3 Rf8

No. 149
1 Q b3 *threat* 2 Q e6
      Sd7; 2 Pe8(S)
      Sd5; 2 Sc4
      Bf7; 2 P × B(Q)
      R × P ck; 2 Pc7

No. 150
1 Q a2 *threat* 2 Q e6
      Sd7; 2 Pe8(S)
      Sd5; 2 Sc4
      Bf7; 2 P × B(Q)
      R × P ck; 2 Pc7

No. 151
1 Q f5 *threat* 2 Q d3
      Sc3–e4; 2 S × S
      Sf6–e4; 2 S × S
      Pe4; 2 Sb6
      Pf3; 2 Se3
      Pb2; 2 R × S

No. 152
1 Rh3 *threat* 2 Q d3
      Sc3–e4; 2 S × S
      Sf6–e4; 2 S × S
      Pe4; 2 Sb6
      Pf3; 2 Se3

No. 153 and 154
1 Ba2 *threat* 2 Rd5
      Bc4, c6; 2 Q b8
      Bd3; 2 Q h2
      Sc4; 2 Q × Bb5
      Sd3; 2 Q e2

No. 155
1 Kb4 *threat* 2 Rd5
      Bc6, e6; 2 Q a7
      Bf5; 2 Q g1
      Se6; 2 Q × Bd7
      Sf5; 2 Q g4

Index

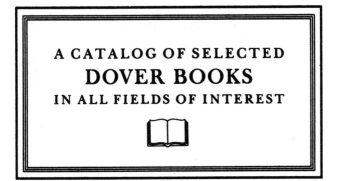

A CATALOG OF SELECTED
DOVER BOOKS
IN ALL FIELDS OF INTEREST

A CATALOG OF SELECTED DOVER
BOOKS IN ALL FIELDS OF INTEREST

CONCERNING THE SPIRITUAL IN ART, Wassily Kandinsky. Pioneering work by father of abstract art. Thoughts on color theory, nature of art. Analysis of earlier masters. 12 illustrations. 80pp. of text. 5⅜ × 8½. 23411-8 Pa. $3.95

ANIMALS: 1,419 Copyright-Free Illustrations of Mammals, Birds, Fish, Insects, etc., Jim Harter (ed.). Clear wood engravings present, in extremely lifelike poses, over 1,000 species of animals. One of the most extensive pictorial sourcebooks of its kind. Captions. Index. 284pp. 9 × 12. 23766-4 Pa. $11.95

CELTIC ART: The Methods of Construction, George Bain. Simple geometric techniques for making Celtic interlacements, spirals, Kells-type initials, animals, humans, etc. Over 500 illustrations. 160pp. 9 × 12. (USO) 22923-8 Pa. $9.95

AN ATLAS OF ANATOMY FOR ARTISTS, Fritz Schider. Most thorough reference work on art anatomy in the world. Hundreds of illustrations, including selections from works by Vesalius, Leonardo, Goya, Ingres, Michelangelo, others. 593 illustrations. 192pp. 7⅛ × 10¼. 20241-0 Pa. $8.95

CELTIC HAND STROKE-BY-STROKE (Irish Half-Uncial from "The Book of Kells"): An Arthur Baker Calligraphy Manual, Arthur Baker. Complete guide to creating each letter of the alphabet in distinctive Celtic manner. Covers hand position, strokes, pens, inks, paper, more. Illustrated. 48pp. 8¼ × 11.
24336-2 Pa. $3.95

EASY ORIGAMI, John Montroll. Charming collection of 32 projects (hat, cup, pelican, piano, swan, many more) specially designed for the novice origami hobbyist. Clearly illustrated easy-to-follow instructions insure that even beginning papercrafters will achieve successful results. 48pp. 8¼ × 11. 27298-2 Pa. $2.95

THE COMPLETE BOOK OF BIRDHOUSE CONSTRUCTION FOR WOOD-WORKERS, Scott D. Campbell. Detailed instructions, illustrations, tables. Also data on bird habitat and instinct patterns. Bibliography. 3 tables. 63 illustrations in 15 figures. 48pp. 5¼ × 8½. 24407-5 Pa. $1.95

BLOOMINGDALE'S ILLUSTRATED 1886 CATALOG: Fashions, Dry Goods and Housewares, Bloomingdale Brothers. Famed merchants' extremely rare catalog depicting about 1,700 products: clothing, housewares, firearms, dry goods, jewelry, more. Invaluable for dating, identifying vintage items. Also, copyright-free graphics for artists, designers. Co-published with Henry Ford Museum & Green-field Village. 160pp. 8¼ × 11. 25780-0 Pa. $9.95

HISTORIC COSTUME IN PICTURES, Braun & Schneider. Over 1,450 costumed figures in clearly detailed engravings—from dawn of civilization to end of 19th century. Captions. Many folk costumes. 256pp. 8⅜ × 11¾. 23150-X Pa. $11.95

CATALOG OF DOVER BOOKS

STICKLEY CRAFTSMAN FURNITURE CATALOGS, Gustav Stickley and L. & J. G. Stickley. Beautiful, functional furniture in two authentic catalogs from 1910. 594 illustrations, including 277 photos, show settles, rockers, armchairs, reclining chairs, bookcases, desks, tables. 183pp. 6½ × 9¼. 23838-5 Pa. $8.95

AMERICAN LOCOMOTIVES IN HISTORIC PHOTOGRAPHS: 1858 to 1949, Ron Ziel (ed.). A rare collection of 126 meticulously detailed official photographs, called "builder portraits," of American locomotives that majestically chronicle the rise of steam locomotive power in America. Introduction. Detailed captions. xi + 129pp. 9 × 12. 27393-8 Pa. $12.95

AMERICA'S LIGHTHOUSES: An Illustrated History, Francis Ross Holland, Jr. Delightfully written, profusely illustrated fact-filled survey of over 200 American lighthouses since 1716. History, anecdotes, technological advances, more. 240pp. 8 × 10¾. 25576-X Pa. $11.95

TOWARDS A NEW ARCHITECTURE, Le Corbusier. Pioneering manifesto by founder of "International School." Technical and aesthetic theories, views of industry, economics, relation of form to function, "mass-production split" and much more. Profusely illustrated. 320pp. 6⅛ × 9¼. (USO) 25023-7 Pa. $8.95

HOW THE OTHER HALF LIVES, Jacob Riis. Famous journalistic record, exposing poverty and degradation of New York slums around 1900, by major social reformer. 100 striking and influential photographs. 233pp. 10 × 7⅞.
22012-5 Pa $10.95

FRUIT KEY AND TWIG KEY TO TREES AND SHRUBS, William M. Harlow. One of the handiest and most widely used identification aids. Fruit key covers 120 deciduous and evergreen species; twig key 160 deciduous species. Easily used. Over 300 photographs. 126pp. 5⅜ × 8½. 20511-8 Pa. $3.95

COMMON BIRD SONGS, Dr. Donald J. Borror. Songs of 60 most common U.S. birds: robins, sparrows, cardinals, bluejays, finches, more—arranged in order of increasing complexity. Up to 9 variations of songs of each species.
Cassette and manual 99911-4 $8.95

ORCHIDS AS HOUSE PLANTS, Rebecca Tyson Northen. Grow cattleyas and many other kinds of orchids—in a window, in a case, or under artificial light. 63 illustrations. 148pp. 5⅜ × 8½. 23261-1 Pa. $3.95

MONSTER MAZES, Dave Phillips. Masterful mazes at four levels of difficulty. Avoid deadly perils and evil creatures to find magical treasures. Solutions for all 32 exciting illustrated puzzles. 48pp. 8¼ × 11. 26005-4 Pa. $2.95

MOZART'S DON GIOVANNI (DOVER OPERA LIBRETTO SERIES), Wolfgang Amadeus Mozart. Introduced and translated by Ellen H. Bleiler. Standard Italian libretto, with complete English translation. Convenient and thoroughly portable—an ideal companion for reading along with a recording or the performance itself. Introduction. List of characters. Plot summary. 121pp. 5¼ × 8½.
24944-1 Pa. $2.95

TECHNICAL MANUAL AND DICTIONARY OF CLASSICAL BALLET, Gail Grant. Defines, explains, comments on steps, movements, poses and concepts. 15-page pictorial section. Basic book for student, viewer. 127pp. 5⅜ × 8½.
21843-0 Pa. $3.95

MY BONDAGE AND MY FREEDOM, Frederick Douglass. Born a slave, Douglass became outspoken force in antislavery movement. The best of Douglass' autobiographies. Graphic description of slave life. 464pp. 5⅜ × 8½. 22457-0 Pa. $8.95

FOLLOWING THE EQUATOR: A Journey Around the World, Mark Twain. Fascinating humorous account of 1897 voyage to Hawaii, Australia, India, New Zealand, etc. Ironic, bemused reports on peoples, customs, climate, flora and fauna, politics, much more. 197 illustrations. 720pp. 5⅜ × 8½. 26113-1 Pa. $15.95

THE PEOPLE CALLED SHAKERS, Edward D. Andrews. Definitive study of Shakers: origins, beliefs, practices, dances, social organization, furniture and crafts, etc. 33 illustrations. 351pp. 5⅜ × 8½. 21081-2 Pa. $8.95

THE MYTHS OF GREECE AND ROME, H. A. Guerber. A classic of mythology, generously illustrated, long prized for its simple, graphic, accurate retelling of the principal myths of Greece and Rome, and for its commentary on their origins and significance. With 64 illustrations by Michelangelo, Raphael, Titian, Rubens, Canova, Bernini and others. 480pp. 5⅜ × 8½. 27584-1 Pa. $9.95

PSYCHOLOGY OF MUSIC, Carl E. Seashore. Classic work discusses music as a medium from psychological viewpoint. Clear treatment of physical acoustics, auditory apparatus, sound perception, development of musical skills, nature of musical feeling, host of other topics. 88 figures. 408pp. 5⅜ × 8½. 21851-1 Pa. $9.95

THE PHILOSOPHY OF HISTORY, Georg W. Hegel. Great classic of Western thought develops concept that history is not chance but rational process, the evolution of freedom. 457pp. 5⅜ × 8½. 20112-0 Pa. $9.95

THE BOOK OF TEA, Kakuzo Okakura. Minor classic of the Orient: entertaining, charming explanation, interpretation of traditional Japanese culture in terms of tea ceremony. 94pp. 5⅜ × 8½. 20070-1 Pa. $2.95

LIFE IN ANCIENT EGYPT, Adolf Erman. Fullest, most thorough, detailed older account with much not in more recent books, domestic life, religion, magic, medicine, commerce, much more. Many illustrations reproduce tomb paintings, carvings, hieroglyphs, etc. 597pp. 5⅜ × 8½. 22632-8 Pa. $10.95

SUNDIALS, Their Theory and Construction, Albert Waugh. Far and away the best, most thorough coverage of ideas, mathematics concerned, types, construction, adjusting anywhere. Simple, nontechnical treatment allows even children to build several of these dials. Over 100 illustrations. 230pp. 5⅜ × 8½. 22947-5 Pa. $7.95

DYNAMICS OF FLUIDS IN POROUS MEDIA, Jacob Bear. For advanced students of ground water hydrology, soil mechanics and physics, drainage and irrigation engineering, and more. 335 illustrations. Exercises, with answers. 784pp. 6⅛ × 9¼. 65675-6 Pa. $19.95

SONGS OF EXPERIENCE: Facsimile Reproduction with 26 Plates in Full Color, William Blake. 26 full-color plates from a rare 1826 edition. Includes "The Tyger," "London," "Holy Thursday," and other poems. Printed text of poems. 48pp. 5¼ × 7. 24636-1 Pa. $4.95

OLD-TIME VIGNETTES IN FULL COLOR, Carol Belanger Grafton (ed.). Over 390 charming, often sentimental illustrations, selected from archives of Victorian graphics—pretty women posing, children playing, food, flowers, kittens and puppies, smiling cherubs, birds and butterflies, much more. All copyright-free. 48pp. 9¼ × 12¼. 27269-9 Pa. $5.95

PERSPECTIVE FOR ARTISTS, Rex Vicat Cole. Depth, perspective of sky and sea, shadows, much more, not usually covered. 391 diagrams, 81 reproductions of drawings and paintings. 279pp. 5⅜ × 8½. 22487-2 Pa. $6.95

DRAWING THE LIVING FIGURE, Joseph Sheppard. Innovative approach to artistic anatomy focuses on specifics of surface anatomy, rather than muscles and bones. Over 170 drawings of live models in front, back and side views, and in widely varying poses. Accompanying diagrams. 177 illustrations. Introduction. Index. 144pp. 8⅜ × 11¼. 26723-7 Pa. $7.95

GOTHIC AND OLD ENGLISH ALPHABETS: 100 Complete Fonts, Dan X. Solo. Add power, elegance to posters, signs, other graphics with 100 stunning copyright-free alphabets: Blackstone, Dolbey, Germania, 97 more—including many lower-case, numerals, punctuation marks. 104pp. 8⅛ × 11. 24695-7 Pa. $7.95

HOW TO DO BEADWORK, Mary White. Fundamental book on craft from simple projects to five-bead chains and woven works. 106 illustrations. 142pp. 5⅜ × 8. 20697-1 Pa. $4.95

THE BOOK OF WOOD CARVING, Charles Marshall Sayers. Finest book for beginners discusses fundamentals and offers 34 designs. "Absolutely first rate . . . well thought out and well executed."—E. J. Tangerman. 118pp. 7¾ × 10⅝. 23654-4 Pa. $5.95

ILLUSTRATED CATALOG OF CIVIL WAR MILITARY GOODS: Union Army Weapons, Insignia, Uniform Accessories, and Other Equipment, Schuyler, Hartley, and Graham. Rare, profusely illustrated 1846 catalog includes Union Army uniform and dress regulations, arms and ammunition, coats, insignia, flags, swords, rifles, etc. 226 illustrations. 160pp. 9 × 12. 24939-5 Pa. $10.95

WOMEN'S FASHIONS OF THE EARLY 1900s: An Unabridged Republication of "New York Fashions, 1909," National Cloak & Suit Co. Rare catalog of mail-order fashions documents women's and children's clothing styles shortly after the turn of the century. Captions offer full descriptions, prices. Invaluable resource for fashion, costume historians. Approximately 725 illustrations. 128pp. 8⅜ × 11¼. 27276-1 Pa. $11.95

THE 1912 AND 1915 GUSTAV STICKLEY FURNITURE CATALOGS, Gustav Stickley. With over 200 detailed illustrations and descriptions, these two catalogs are essential reading and reference materials and identification guides for Stickley furniture. Captions cite materials, dimensions and prices. 112pp. 6½ × 9¼. 26676-1 Pa. $9.95

EARLY AMERICAN LOCOMOTIVES, John H. White, Jr. Finest locomotive engravings from early 19th century: historical (1804–74), main-line (after 1870), special, foreign, etc. 147 plates. 142pp. 11⅜ × 8¼. 22772-3 Pa. $8.95

THE TALL SHIPS OF TODAY IN PHOTOGRAPHS, Frank O. Braynard. Lavishly illustrated tribute to nearly 100 majestic contemporary sailing vessels: Amerigo Vespucci, Clearwater, Constitution, Eagle, Mayflower, Sea Cloud, Victory, many more. Authoritative captions provide statistics, background on each ship. 190 black-and-white photographs and illustrations. Introduction. 128pp. 8⅞ × 11¾. 27163-3 Pa. $13.95

BRASS INSTRUMENTS: Their History and Development, Anthony Baines. Authoritative, updated survey of the evolution of trumpets, trombones, bugles, cornets, French horns, tubas and other brass wind instruments. Over 140 illustrations and 48 music examples. Corrected and updated by author. New preface. Bibliography. 320pp. 5⅜ × 8½. 27574-4 Pa. $9.95

HOLLYWOOD GLAMOR PORTRAITS, John Kobal (ed.). 145 photos from 1926–49. Harlow, Gable, Bogart, Bacall; 94 stars in all. Full background on photographers, technical aspects. 160pp. 8⅜ × 11¼. 23352-9 Pa. $11.95

MAX AND MORITZ, Wilhelm Busch. Great humor classic in both German and English. Also 10 other works: "Cat and Mouse," "Plisch and Plumm," etc. 216pp. 5⅜ × 8½. 20181-3 Pa. $5.95

THE RAVEN AND OTHER FAVORITE POEMS, Edgar Allan Poe. Over 40 of the author's most memorable poems: "The Bells," "Ulalume," "Israfel," "To Helen," "The Conqueror Worm," "Eldorado," "Annabel Lee," many more. Alphabetic lists of titles and first lines. 64pp. 5³⁄₁₆ × 8¼. 26685-0 Pa. $1.00

SEVEN SCIENCE FICTION NOVELS, H. G. Wells. The standard collection of the great novels. Complete, unabridged. First Men in the Moon, Island of Dr. Moreau, War of the Worlds, Food of the Gods, Invisible Man, Time Machine, In the Days of the Comet. Total of 1,015pp. 5⅜ × 8½. (USO) 20264-X Clothbd. $29.95

AMULETS AND SUPERSTITIONS, E. A. Wallis Budge. Comprehensive discourse on origin, powers of amulets in many ancient cultures: Arab, Persian, Babylonian, Assyrian, Egyptian, Gnostic, Hebrew, Phoenician, Syriac, etc. Covers cross, swastika, crucifix, seals, rings, stones, etc. 584pp. 5⅜ × 8½. 23573-4 Pa. $12.95

RUSSIAN STORIES/PYCCKNE PACCKA3bl: A Dual-Language Book, edited by Gleb Struve. Twelve tales by such masters as Chekhov, Tolstoy, Dostoevsky, Pushkin, others. Excellent word-for-word English translations on facing pages, plus teaching and study aids, Russian/English vocabulary, biographical/critical introductions, more. 416pp. 5⅜ × 8½. 26244-8 Pa. $8.95

PHILADELPHIA THEN AND NOW: 60 Sites Photographed in the Past and Present, Kenneth Finkel and Susan Oyama. Rare photographs of City Hall, Logan Square, Independence Hall, Betsy Ross House, other landmarks juxtaposed with contemporary views. Captures changing face of historic city. Introduction. Captions. 128pp. 8¼ × 11. 25790-8 Pa. $9.95

AIA ARCHITECTURAL GUIDE TO NASSAU AND SUFFOLK COUNTIES, LONG ISLAND, The American Institute of Architects, Long Island Chapter, and the Society for the Preservation of Long Island Antiquities. Comprehensive, well-researched and generously illustrated volume brings to life over three centuries of Long Island's great architectural heritage. More than 240 photographs with authoritative, extensively detailed captions. 176pp. 8¼ × 11. 26946-9 Pa. $14.95

NORTH AMERICAN INDIAN LIFE: Customs and Traditions of 23 Tribes, Elsie Clews Parsons (ed.). 27 fictionalized essays by noted anthropologists examine religion, customs, government, additional facets of life among the Winnebago, Crow, Zuni, Eskimo, other tribes. 480pp. 6⅛ × 9¼. 27377-6 Pa. $10.95

CATALOG OF DOVER BOOKS

THE INFLUENCE OF SEA POWER UPON HISTORY, 1660–1783, A. T. Mahan. Influential classic of naval history and tactics still used as text in war colleges. First paperback edition. 4 maps. 24 battle plans. 640pp. 5⅜ × 8½. 25509-3 Pa. $12.95

THE STORY OF THE TITANIC AS TOLD BY ITS SURVIVORS, Jack Winocour (ed.). What it was really like. Panic, despair, shocking inefficiency, and a little heroism. More thrilling than any fictional account. 26 illustrations. 320pp. 5⅜ × 8½. 20610-6 Pa. $7.95

FAIRY AND FOLK TALES OF THE IRISH PEASANTRY, William Butler Yeats (ed.). Treasury of 64 tales from the twilight world of Celtic myth and legend: "The Soul Cages," "The Kildare Pooka," "King O'Toole and his Goose," many more. Introduction and Notes by W. B. Yeats. 352pp. 5⅜ × 8½. 26941-8 Pa. $8.95

BUDDHIST MAHAYANA TEXTS, E. B. Cowell and Others (eds.). Superb, accurate translations of basic documents in Mahayana Buddhism, highly important in history of religions. The Buddha-karita of Asvaghosha, Larger Sukhavativyuha, more. 448pp. 5⅜ × 8½. 25552-2 Pa. $9.95

ONE TWO THREE . . . INFINITY: Facts and Speculations of Science, George Gamow. Great physicist's fascinating, readable overview of contemporary science: number theory, relativity, fourth dimension, entropy, genes, atomic structure, much more. 128 illustrations. Index. 352pp. 5⅜ × 8½. 25664-2 Pa. $8.95

ENGINEERING IN HISTORY, Richard Shelton Kirby, et al. Broad, nontechnical survey of history's major technological advances: birth of Greek science, industrial revolution, electricity and applied science, 20th-century automation, much more. 181 illustrations. ". . . excellent . . ."—Isis. Bibliography. vii + 530pp. 5⅜ × 8¼. 26412-2 Pa. $14.95

Prices subject to change without notice.

Available at your book dealer or write for free catalog to Dept. GI, Dover Publications, Inc., 31 East 2nd St., Mineola, N.Y. 11501. Dover publishes more than 500 books each year on science, elementary and advanced mathematics, biology, music, art, literary history, social sciences and other areas.